Civil Society

CIVIL SOCIETY

OLD IMAGES, NEW VISIONS

JOHN KEANE

Polity Press

First published in 1998 by Polity Press in association with Blackwell Publishers Ltd.

Editorial office:
Polity Press
65 Bridge Street
Cambridge CB2 1UR, UK

Marketing and production:
Blackwell Publishers Ltd
108 Cowley Road
Oxford OX4 1JF, UK

ISBN 0-7456-2070-1
ISBN 0-7456-2071-X (pbk)

A catalogue record for this book is available from the British Library.

Typeset in 11 on 13 pt Berling by Ace Filmsetting, Frome, Somerset
Printed in Great Britain by T J International, Padstow, Cornwall

This book is printed on acid-free paper.

Contents

Openings

February 1997: Half way through writing this book, a registered letter arrived from a colleague in Belgrade. Chock-full of newspaper clippings, sample posters, postcards and photographs, the tattered package held together in a wrapping of string contained a short letter describing the dramatic, now world-famous Serbian events of the previous several months. 'You should really come to see with your own eyes the wonders of the past 72 days,' the letter began. 'Each evening, during the state-controlled television news programme, thousands of people join in with "noise is fashionable" actions. They fling open their windows and clang pots and pans, or honk their car horns in unison, or assemble peacefully in the streets blowing whistles, clarinets and trumpets. When the programme has ended, the racket stops at once. Thousands of people in small groups then go walking through the frozen streets of Belgrade. Police cordons are simply unable to stop them, especially because the students form "cordons against cordons", and because the numbers of walkers grow as each day passes.'

'Walking is important to us', the letter continued. 'It symbolizes our reclaiming of space, our new civil freedoms. Routes and gathering points are usually decided and coordinated by mobile phone. We walk everywhere that we can: around the courtyard of the university rectorate, past the education ministry and the offices of *Politika*, over to the egg-splattered premises of Serbian Television. Sometimes the marchers walk in circles, acting like prisoners. The weather is unusually cold here. Minus ten or worse. Sympathizers supply the walkers with food, tea and coffee. Student organizations urge everybody to avoid alcohol. There have also been many huge demonstrations in Republic Square, with flowers, whistles, placards, flags, gleeful children, costumes, musicians, actors, dancing, the singing of patriotic hymns. The demonstrators don't forget that they live in the Balkans. They have a lot to say about nationalism and war, lawlessness and pauperization. But they also sense that there are signs in everyday life, especially within families, cultural and educational organizations, that decency, openness and autonomous personality formation have survived. Perhaps that is why, through all of these dramas, our President and his Lady Macbeth have kept silent and remained invisible. They surely have a whiff of what they cannot stomach: a civil society is emerging in their land.'

September 1997: As this book neared completion, Dr Mahathir bin Muhammad, Prime Minister of Malaysia, delivered a conference speech to showcase his country's new Multimedia Super Corridor (MSC).[1] Extending north from Malaysia's new international airport to the city of Kuala Lumpur, now dominated by the soaring Petronas twin towers, the MSC is a 15-by-50 kilometre zone which symbolizes Malaysia's commitment to a future based on the new revolution in digital communications technology, Dr Mahathir explained. He described how the dedicated zone will offer the companies which invest in it state-of-the-art facilities, enabling them to expand their frontiers through electronic commerce, smart partnerships with global IT leaders, and capital-raising ventures on the Internet. MSC will incorporate an intelligent city, Cyberjaya, and a new 'wired' federal capital, Putrajaya, Dr Mahathir added. He went on to report that the first futuristic building, 'Cyberview', has been completed, that the construction of the Multimedia University is soon scheduled for com-

---

[1] Dr Mahathir bin Muhammad, 'Inventing our Common Future', a speech delivered to the Multimedia Asia 1997 (MMA '97) Conference and Exhibition at The Mines Resort City, Seri Kembangan, Malaysia (16 September 1997).

pletion, and that more than 40 Malaysian and foreign companies – including US giant Microsoft, whose founder Bill Gates sits on the MSC's international advisory panel – have made firm commitments to the project.

Pointing out that the MSC is an integral part of his broader Vision 2020 masterplan, Dr Mahathir pledged in his speech to lead his country into the Information Age by fostering 'electronic government'. Its priorities include 'paperless' government offices and automated government procurement. Electronic government would also embrace more transparent, effective and efficient delivery of services to citizens – for instance, the development of one-stop service windows, through which citizens can go to a kiosk in a shopping mall or use a PC at home to renew their driving licences or pay their electricity bills in one simple session. Electronic government would prove to be lean government, Dr Mahathir predicted. 'The government expenditure is not very big. The private sector will put in the infrastructure,' he said, before making another prediction that the primary long-term impact of the Multimedia Super Corridor would be felt underneath government, in the social domain. Not only would the MSC serve to create such new services and products as the world's first wallet-sized, multifunction computer called 'e-pass'. The transformation of Malaysia into a knowledge-based society through information technology would spread into the everyday lives of Malaysians. 'We want to become a developed nation in our own mould,' concluded Dr Mahathir. 'Malaysia's IT agenda defines the content of the mould as the creation of a civil society. By civil society we mean a community which is self-regulating and empowered through the use of knowledge, skills and values inculcated within the people. Such a society will allow every Malaysian to live a life of managed destiny and dignity, not just in the here and now, but also in the hereafter.'

Power

Political events sketched in a personal letter from Belgrade and a formal speech by a key politician of a far-distant, newly industrializing country appear to have nothing in common, except for two words: civil society. Given the contemporary popularity of the phrase, the overlap is both significant and unsurprising. For nearly a century and a half, the language of civil society virtually disappeared from intellectual and political life, and, as recently as a decade ago, the language of civil society remained strange sounding, quite unfashionable, even greeted with cynicism or hostility in certain circles. Since then, in the European region and elsewhere, the term 'civil society' has become so voguish in the human sciences and uttered so often through the lips of politicians, business leaders, academics, foundation executives, relief agencies and citizens, that the even-handed *Times Literary Supplement* has observed, with justification, that 'the very phrase is becoming motherhood-and-apple pie of the 1990s'.[1]

My own research projects on the topic of civil society and the state anticipated this development. They tried to describe and explain its contours to observers who found the whole development surprising or puzzling, because they lived either in contexts (such as Russia) where until recently the equivalent term 'civil society' had never existed; or in contexts (like the United States) where virtually the same theme of civil

[1] *Times Literary Supplement*, no. 4940 (5 December 1997), p. 30.

society had been addressed under the different, but none-
theless overlapping (but arguably less fecund) debate concerning the political dangers of citizens' declining capacity
for organizing themselves into groups – their tendency to go
'bowling alone' – and the philosophical and political merits of
'communitarianism' and 'liberalism'. My projects on civil society were conceived in quite different circumstances. They originally grew out of a study of the attempt to retrieve the concept
of the public sphere (*Öffentlichkeit*) in twentieth-century German political thought from the time of Max Weber.[2] The research was also nurtured by several practical commitments: for
instance, in the underground university and civic initiatives in
Czechoslovakia; my public engagement with the intellectual
and political controversies produced by the collapsing welfare
state project; and the work of drafting and launching Charter
88, a citizens' initiative that called publicly for a written constitution for Britain. The research projects on civil society and
the state were eventually published in 1988 – and republished
a decade later – as a two-volume contribution entitled *Democracy and Civil Society* and *Civil Society and the State: New European Perspectives*.[3] These books aimed to stir up new discussions
about an old-fashioned category, to invest it with fresh theoretical meaning and political significance. The volumes posed
questions that continue to resonate in our times: What precisely is meant by the originally eighteenth-century distinction
between the state and the non-state realm of civil society? Why
has that distinction, so crucial throughout the first half of the
nineteenth century and then apparently lost without trace, again
become sharply topical? For what intellectual and political
purposes can the distinction be used and whose intellectual
and political interests might it serve?

For various reasons, some of them masking my own intellectual weaknesses, *Democracy and Civil Society* and *Civil Society
and the State* came to be considered 'classics' in their field. It is

[2] *Public Life and Late Capitalism* (Cambridge and New York, 1984).
[3] *Democracy and Civil Society: On the Predicaments of European Socialism, the
Prospects for Democracy, and the Problem of Controlling Social and Political
Power* (London and New York, 1988; London, 1998); *Civil Society and the
State: New European Perspectives* (London and New York, 1988; London, 1998).

worth reflecting for a moment on these two works, since the
'old images' they contain help us today to make sense of the
'new versions' of civil society that can and should be developed during the coming years. *Democracy and Civil Society* and
Civil Society and the State examined the late-eighteenth-century European origins and early-nineteenth-century development of the distinction between civil society and the state.
These works showed that the language of civil society (*societas civilis*), traditionally used to speak of a peaceful political
order governed by law, came instead to refer to a realm of life
institutionally separated from territorial state institutions. The
volumes emphasized the ways in which, during the period
1750–1850, the language of civil society became fragile and
polysemic, an object of intensive discussion and controversy.
From the time of the American Revolution, it was argued,
many writers used the term 'civil society', admittedly in a variety of confused ways, to refer to dynamic webs of interre-
lated non-governmental institutions, such as market economies,
households, charitable groups, clubs and voluntary associations,
independent churches and publishing houses. The two volumes invested much effort in the philosophical task of recon-
structing and building upon these early modern understandings
of civil society. Civil society, as I used the term and still do, is
an ideal-typical category (an *idealtyp* in the sense of Max Weber) that both describes and envisages a complex and dynamic
ensemble of legally protected non-governmental institutions
that tend to be non-violent, self-organizing, self-reflexive, and
permanently in tension with each other and with the state
institutions that 'frame', constrict and enable their activities.

   Civil Society and the State and *Democracy and Civil Society*
tried to illustrate just how useful this term is when analysing
past events – like the uneven geographic distribution of abso-
lutist states, or the emergence of modern forms of exclusion
of women from public life, or the 'civilizing' of European manners. And emphasis was placed upon the capacity of the old-
fashioned theoretical distinction between civil society and state
institutions to make new and different sense of contemporary
social and political developments. For instance, *Democracy and
Civil Society* and *Civil Society and the State* showed why the

resistance to totalitarian regimes after the crushing of the Prague Spring often spoke the language of civil society. But these books insisted that the state–civil society distinction is not only vitally important in contexts lacking basic political and civil freedoms. The language of civil society, they argued, applies equally well to such disparate political phenomena as the decline of the welfare state, the rise of neo-liberalism and the growth of social movements. In this way, these two volumes anticipated, and tried to counter, the lingering suspicion that the civil society perspective has been overtaken by late-twentieth-century events; that the concept of civil society perhaps proved useful in the development of critical analyses of despotism, and in projects of mobilizing politically against it, but that the concept is now much less helpful when it comes to thinking and acting constructively about how to organize 'late modern' democratic institutions.

* * *

Various arguments were mustered against the prejudice and suspicion that the language of civil society has become obsolete. The case *for* civil society was wide ranging. It included the argument that a civil society gives preferential treatment to individuals' daily freedom from violence; claims concerning the importance of enabling groups and individuals freely within the law to define and express their various social identities; the argument that freedom of communication is impossible without networks of variously sized non-state communications media; and (an argument that is extended below) the insistence that politically regulated and socially constrained markets are superior devices for eliminating all those factors of production that fail to perform according to current standards of efficiency. But of special interest to both volumes was the subject of democracy or, more precisely, the intellectual and political need to revive the democratic imagination. In countering the suspicion that civil society is an *idée passée*, the volumes strived to think unconventionally and constructively about the optimal conditions under which the modern democratic tradition can survive and flourish globally after a century marked by revolutionary upheavals, total war, totalitarianism and welfare state *dirigisme*.

These volumes understood democracy as a special type of political system in which civil society and state institutions tend to function as two necessary moments, separate but contiguous, distinct but interdependent, internal articulations of a system in which the exercise of power, whether in the household or the corporate boardroom and government office, is subject to public disputation, compromise and agreement.

This revised understanding of democracy rejected the narrow complacency of those who consider it as simply government by means of periodic elections, party competition, majority rule and the rule of law. The volumes argued for the growing importance of considering not only *who* votes in elections but *where* people vote and, thus, for the incorporation into democratic politics of 'social life' as a possible domain of democratization. Partly under the influence of my working contacts with the post-totalitarian regimes of Czechoslovakia, Poland and Yugoslavia, *Democracy and Civil Society* went further. It attempted to stake out a new *democratic* interpretation of democracy, one that is more genuinely *pluralist*, philosophically and politically speaking. The proposed account of democracy rejected the arrogant search for ultimate Truth and ultimate Solutions. It called into question our bad habit of worshipping so-called universal imperatives and of riding rough-shod over contingencies. Both books argued that democratic theories of politics must resist the temptation to attribute universal importance to particular ways of life. Priority is to be given to avoiding the alarming tendency – evident in the political wreckage left behind by the twentieth century – to boss ourselves and others, using sticks and stones and ideologies, into accepting our preferred version of the world. This is best done, the two volumes proposed, by redefining democracy as the institutionalized duty to doubt calls to worship Grand Ideals, as the obligation to defend greater pluralism, and as the emphasis on institutional complexity and public accountability as barriers against dangerous accumulations of power, wherever and whenever they develop.

The commitment to pluralism and power sharing in *Democracy and Civil Society* and *Civil Society and the State* was in turn linked conceptually to the argument for a forward-looking democratic politics with eyes in the back of its head. Convinced that in matters concerning democracy the past is crucial for the present; that tradition is not the private property of conservatives; and that (as Jean Starobinski has famously insisted) a key element of a modernist outlook is the presence of the past in the present that attempts constantly to claim and supersede the past, the two volumes tried to convince readers that the viability of democratic theory and politics depends *not* on their capacity to forget about the past, but at least in part on their ability to retrieve, reconstruct and imaginatively transform old, but unexhausted political languages in markedly changed circumstances. That exercise in what Walter Benjamin called *rettende Kritik* was evident in the repeated references to the social and political thought of the age of the democratic revolution – to the period in Europe after 1760, when old loyalties snapped and many people experienced obedience to existing power as a form of humiliation. In particular, *Civil Society and the State* and *Democracy and Civil Society* were preoccupied with rescuing the early modern awareness of the difference between 'society' and 'state' from the condescension of posterity. The two volumes tried to make the originally eighteenth-century distinction between civil society and the state call and dance to the tunes of contemporary politics. The volumes emphasized that the process of democratization cannot be synonymous with the extension of total state power into the non-state sphere of civil society. Conversely, they emphasized that democratization cannot be defined as the abolition of the state and the building of spontaneous agreement among citizens living within civil society. The unending project of democracy, it was argued, must steer a course between these two unworkable extremes. Democracy is an always difficult, permanently extended process of apportioning and publicly monitoring the exercise of power within polities marked by the institutionally distinct – but always mediated – realms of civil society and state institutions.

* * *

When viewed from the perspective of democratic theory and politics, *Civil Society and the State* and *Democracy and Civil Society* were not only attempts to stimulate discussion about the contemporary utility of certain old eighteenth- and early nineteenth-century images of civil society. They also tried to retrieve and critically develop this period's remarkable insights into the perennial problem of how publicly to apportion and control the exercise of power. Those books prefigured, and are linked to, two subsequent works: *The Media and Democracy* (1991), which thinks with and against certain eighteenth-century trends to ask questions about the contemporary political functions of communications media; and *Tom Paine: A Political Life* (1995), which is a study of the life and times of democratic republicanism in the Atlantic region during the second half of the eighteenth century. All four works are bound together by the thought that public suspicion of power in its various forms is an essential ingredient of our early modern democratic heritage. In the American colonies prior to 1776, for example, a great deal of the literature that poured from the presses of printing shops supposed a theory of politics that is strikingly relevant, so much so that it feels linked to our times in the most intimate way. Many colonists worked from the idea that the driving force behind every political development, the key determinant of every political controversy, is power. Power was understood as the exercise of dominion by some men over the lives of others, and it was seen as a permanent temptation in human affairs. Likened most often to the act of trespassing, power was said to have an 'encroaching' nature, like a beast bent on devouring its natural prey: liberty, law or right. The key problem in human affairs, this literature implied, was how to preserve liberty by inventing effective checks on the wielders of power, apportioning and monitoring it, ensuring its responsible exercise.

⌐*Democracy and Civil Society* and *Civil Society and the State* did not embrace the naturalistic imagery of power as a beast, but in attempting to rescue and revive the early modern sensitivity to power the two volumes were able to suggest that a revised theory of democracy could meet head-on the dominant tendency in western political thought to define political systems as power-ridden relationships between superiors and inferiors.⌐The history of political thought has been mainly a history written from above. The dominant tradition that runs from Plato's *Statesman* and Xenophon's *Cyropaedia* to Hobbes's *Leviathan* and Schmitt's *Die Diktatur* has represented political power from the standpoint of the rulers. It has sought to justify the power-holders' right to command and the subjects' duty to obey by defending various principles of legitimacy, including the authority of God; the will of the people; nature (as an original force, *kratos*, or as the law of reason or modern natural law) and appeals to history; or, as in legal positivism, by emphasizing the fact of existing laws that are made and enforced by authorities appointed by the political system itself. This dominant tradition has, of course, come under fire increasingly in modern times. The entitlements of the governed – the dark side of the moon of western political thought – have come ever more sharply in focus. The natural rights of the individual; the liberty, wealth and happiness of citizens; the right of resistance to unjust laws; the separation of powers; liberty of the press; the rule of law; office holding and law making subject to time limits: these and other principles, which are seen to exist independently of political power, which is required both to respect and to protect them, have been invoked in opposition to oligarchic and state-centred theories of politics. *Democracy and Civil Society* and *Civil Society and the State* aimed to retrieve, reconstruct and develop the power-sharing 'spirit' of such principles. They did so principally by insisting that the exercise of power is best monitored and controlled publicly within a democratic order marked by the institutional separation of civil society and state institutions. Seen from this power-sharing perspective, state actors and institutions within a democracy are constantly forced to respect, protect and share power with civilian actors and institutions – just as civilians living within the state-protected institutions of a heterogeneous civil society are forced to recognize social differences and to share power among themselves. A democracy, in short, was seen as a fractured and self-reflexive system of power in which there are daily reminders to governors and governed alike that those who exercise power over others cannot do anything they want, and that (as Spinoza put it) even sovereigns are forced in practice to recognize that they cannot make a table eat grass.

Global trends

Civil Society and the State and *Democracy and Civil Society* were among those lucky books that are held aloft after launch by warm winds of opinion. These works fought hard to retrieve the state–civil society distinction from the bookshelves of the distant past. Judging by their buoyant sales and many scores of reviews, translations, interviews, replies and even pirated editions, they helped in a modest way to popularize the category of civil society and to bring it to the heart of various branches of the human sciences. Other works on the subject had, of course, appeared before mine: for instance, in Latin America, where a neo-Gramscian account of the concept of civil society was used as a theoretical weapon against dictatorship;[1] and even earlier still in Japan, where (unknown to me at the time) the contemporary renewal of the language of civil society and the state first began during the second half of the 1960s, especially thanks to the work of the so-called Civil Society School of Japanese Marxism.[2]

---

[1] See Caterina Mengotti, 'Civil Society in the Latin American Context', unpublished paper, Centre for the Study of Democracy (London, January 1998); Carlos Nelson Coutinho, 'As categorias de Gramsci e a realidad brasileira', *Presenca* (Rio de Janeiro, 8 September 1986), pp. 141–62; Norbert Lechner, 'De la révolution de la democratie (le débat intellectuel en Amérique du Sud)', *Esprit* (July 1986), pp. 1–13; and Guillermo O'Donnell and Philippe C. Schmitter, 'Resurrecting Civil Society', in *Transition from Authoritarian Rule: Tentative Conclusions about Uncertain Democracies* (Baltimore, 1986), pp. 48–56.

[2] The main works include Yoshihiko Uchida, *Nihon Shihonshugi no Shiso-zo*

What might be called phase one of the contemporary renaissance of civil society is evident in the writings of Yoshihiko
Uchida and Kiyoaki Hirata, who used the term 'civil society'
(*shimin-shakai*) in a neo-Gramscian sense to highlight three
themes. First, emphasis was placed on the importance, in the
Japanese context, of breaking the bad habit of relying upon
European social science concepts and methods that were seen
to be wooden, with insufficient resonance in the everyday lives
of individuals. So Uchida positively called for a new, less academic social science, sensitive to the need for 'compassion with
toiling people'[3] within the sphere of civil society. Secondly,
the concept of civil society was used to deepen the analysis of
the peculiarities of Japanese capitalism. Without saying so, the
Civil Society School of Japanese Marxism developed an early
version of what later would be called 'the Asian values argument'. Particular emphasis was placed upon the survival in
modern Japan of unusually strong premodern sentiments, such
as communalism, patriarchal family life and individuals' deference towards power. The *weakness* of civil society, in the
sense of shared social networks that infuse individuals with a
strong sense of their individuality, enabled Japanese capitalism to grow at an exceptional speed without significant social
resistance. In consequence, the demands imposed by capital
were more easily realizable and to the detriment of civil liberties, such as the entitlement to improved living, working and
environmental conditions.

Seen from this perspective, Japanese capitalism has been a
form of capitalism without a civil society – note the refusal to
conflate the two categories – and this peculiar weakness of
civil society, it was argued, helped explain the unusually ma-
nipulative, authoritarian quality of the Japanese state, despite
the introduction of American-style democracy following mili-

[Images of Japanese Capitalism through the Social Sciences] (Tokyo, 1967)
and two works by Kiyoaki Hirata, *Shimin-shakai to Shakaishugi* [Civil
Society and Socialism] (Tokyo, 1969) and *Keizaigaku to Rekishi-ninshiki*
[Political Economy and Philosophy of History] (Tokyo, 1971). I am most
grateful to my colleague Takashi Inoguchi for advice about these works.
[3] Yoshihiko Uchida, *Nihon Shihonshugi no Shiso-zo*, op. cit., p. 353.

tary defeat. Whereas in western Europe the primacy of civil rights over the state is a given axiom, in Japan, argued Uchida, the 'rights of the State' are presumed to be primary. This leads to a third point: the problem of overbloated state power, it was argued, has reached crisis proportions in the Soviet model of socialism, in which the state is omnipotent and civil society is impotent. Existing socialist countries need to develop civil societies, if only to actualize the basic ideal, outlined by Marx in the *Grundrisse der Kritik der politischen Ökonomie*, and at the end of Book I of *Das Kapital*, of 'social individuality'. Socialism stands for nothing, argued Hirata, unless it establishes a new system of property relations in which individuals can realize their various potentials by means of their labour, in cooperation with other social individuals. Socialism must be self-managed socialism.

*   *   *

Phase one of the contemporary renaissance of civil society was short-lived. Although the Civil Society School of Japanese Marxism attracted some controversy, it was confined to its country of origin. Its influence was weak, in no small measure because its talk of self-managing socialism arguably short-circuited, or spoiled outright, the democratic potential of the novel emphasis upon civil society. The unoriginal vision of self-regulating socialism was also deeply problematic, especially because it shared with classical Marxism a certain faith in the goal of creating a communist society without class divisions, and thus without the modern division between the state and civil society. Insofar as it was ultimately driven by the reverie of abolishing civil society by means of civil society, the Civil Society School of Japanese Marxism was undermined by its deep dependence upon the Gramscian approach, which emphasizes the tactical importance of non-market, non-state institutions in the struggle against the exploitative power of capitalist society.

The strengths and weaknesses of the Gramscian approach are worth reviewing in any effort to reconsider old images and new visions of civil society. Against narrow-minded trade unionism, with its preoccupation with struggles at the point of production, Gramsci proposed, mainly in his prison note-books, that the grip of the property-owning class is most vul-nerable within the cultural institutions of civil society, which otherwise function to 'popularize' and to reproduce among the subordinate classes and groups the dominant bourgeois sense of reality or *egemonia*. Gramsci usually – not always con-sistently – likened civil society to the labyrinthine trench sys-tems of modern warfare. Wedged between the state and class-structured economy – note the unusual geography of Gramsci's account of civil society – these 'fortresses and earthworks' normally protect the 'outer ditch' of state power and shield the ruling class from the shock waves produced by economic crises.

It is precisely the complexity of civil society that enables those who are well organized and cunning to penetrate its manifold structures. Gramsci considered that a protracted 'war of position' within the trenches of civil society could under-mine the power of the bourgeoisie within its home territories of the economy and the coercive state. Seen in this way, the empowerment of the subordinated classes, especially 'the fun-damental class' of the proletariat, depends vitally upon the prior capturing of civil society. Gramsci here attacked the Bolshevik strategy of violently seizing state power. The key aim of the proletarian 'war of position' is to avoid 'statolatry' by creating a *communist* civil society, whose successive enlarge-ment would undermine the foundations of state and class power, thus sidestepping the danger of political dictatorship that would certainly result from a sudden frontal assault upon the state apparatus, or what Gramsci called a 'war of move-ment'.

* * *

The Gramscian approach may continue to have a certain in-tuitive appeal. And it is true that its rejection of 'economism' and its highlighting of the co-dependence of economies and states upon sociocultural institutions are important. It is never-theless hopelessly flawed in several respects. To begin with, social and political conditions in the core capitalist countries have changed so dramatically since Gramsci's time that his thesis of the 'leading role of the proletariat' must be rejected. The more recent fragmentation of national labour movements, the decline in the relative size of the 'core' working class due to deindustrialization and the growing prominence of services, challenges to the work ethic, and the growth of a variety of citizens' initiatives and movements – to mention only the more pertinent developments – jeopardize Gramsci's exaggerated belief that the industrial working class ('the fundamental class') must play the leading role in the anti-capitalist revolution. In other words, Gramsci's presumptions that capitalist society is characterized by a central contradiction and that there is a privileged subject capable of fulfilling the *telos* of history are both contradicted by the growing complexity and differentiation of power in contemporary capitalist systems.[4]

Gramsci's belief in the leading role of the Communist Party – the Modern Prince – in the struggle for socialism implicitly recognizes these difficulties, but it does not help much. It evidently understates the various factors working against the capacity of the mass political party to organize and integrate civil society into its ranks.[5] It also underestimates the totalitarian potential of monopolistic parties, a suspicion that is fuelled by the reverie of abolishing civil society. Gramsci's strategic interest in civil society is wholly opportunistic. It envisages a future classless 'regulated society', and it therefore draws the political conclusion that civil society is a temporary and historically disposable arrangement. Gramsci's political strategy is driven by the reverie of abolishing civil society by means of civil society.

Despite widespread recognition of these problems, 'sublimated' Gramscian assumptions are evident in some fields of the contemporary human sciences. A case in point is the unfortunate analytic separation of the non-state realm into economy and civil society, evident in the neo-Gramscian ef-

---

[4] The point is admitted in neo-Gramscian writings, such as Ernesto Laclau and Chantal Mouffe, *Hegemony and Socialist Strategy: Towards a Radical Democratic Politics* (London, 1985), especially chapter 4.
[5] See my 'Party-centred Socialism?', in *Democracy and Civil Society*, op. cit., pp. 101–51.

forts of Jürgen Habermas to distinguish between the logics of the political and economic systems, regulated respectively by administrative power and money, and civil society, or the life-world (*Lebenswelt*), which is based (potentially) on rules of solidarity and free and open communication.[6] Concerning matters of production, exchange and consumption, this type of neo-Gramscian approach generates several conceptual difficulties, each carrying strategic implications. Civil society, because it is defined so narrowly, is represented as economically passive, exactly because by definition it is deprived of any property resources which would enable it to defend or expand its power. Workers' campaigns to nurture civil freedoms, like that of early Solidarność in Poland or more recent trade union initiatives against racism in the workplace, are made to appear as a contradiction in terms.

Moreover, because civil society is defined as the realm of (potential) freedom it is viewed positively; by contrast, and by implication, the economy is viewed negatively, as a realm of necessity in which (here there is a close affinity with the neo-liberal view) only money speaks. This view is questionable. Not only are the material conditions of life in any actually existing civil society theoretically degraded to a mere instrument for achieving the ends desired by civil society – in just the same way that the classical Greek concept of civil society presupposed the silent unfreedom of the *oikos*. The vital preconditions of an economy are also read out of the analysis. Whether the error is intended or not, actors within any given economy are presumed, falsely, never to give to charities, never to hold or enjoy social functions, and never to form trade unions or professional and trade associations. Another point is overlooked: that economic actors always and every-

---

[6] See Jürgen Habermas, *Theorie des kommunikativen Handelns* (Frankfurt am Main, 1982), vol. 2, p. 471. Similar difficulties are evident in the approach of Jean L. Cohen and Andrew Arato, *Civil Society and Political Theory* (Cambridge, Mass., 1992). See also my earlier critique in 'Work and the Civilizing Process', in *Democracy and Civil Society: On the Predicaments of European Socialism, the Prospects for Democracy, and the Problem of Controlling Social and Political Power* (London and New York, 1988), pp. 69–100.

where go about their business and do their work, and can only ever do so, if they draw upon *endogenous* sources of 'social capital': that is to say, if 'the economy' of which they are members is 'embedded' in a wider civil society that harbours social interaction based on such norms as trust, reliability, punctuality, honesty, friendship, the capacity for group commitment, and non-violent mutual recognition.

The same point is sometimes put more forcefully: in the most productive post-industrial societies, the need for a lively and flexible civil society of norm-based exchange and informal, decentralized and 'flat' organizations – a *networking civil society* – becomes ever more important as goods and services become more complex and computerized.[7] In effect, this heightened co-dependence of contemporary markets upon other civil society institutions confirms an old rule about the strengths and weaknesses of market forces. On the one hand, economies driven by commodity production and exchange have the great advantage of minimizing collective losses. Market forces ensure that factors of production that fail to perform according to current standards of efficiency are continuously and swiftly eliminated and compelled to find alternative and more productive uses. Market forces continuously ensure that 'uncompetitive' factors of production go to the wall. Markets operate according to Abraham Lincoln's maxim that those who need a helping hand should look no further than the lower end of their right arm. In this way, markets invite the victims of competition to blame themselves – and to survive by adapting to new standards of efficiency.[8] On the other hand – these are the key structural weaknesses

[7] Francis Fukuyama, *The End of Order* (London, 1997), p. 77. See also his *Trust: The Social Virtues and the Creation of Prosperity* (New York, 1995). Relevant here as well are the much-discussed works by Robert D. Putnam, *Making Democracy Work: Civic Traditions in Modern Italy* (Princeton, 1993), and 'Bowling Alone: America's Declining Social Capital', *Journal of Democracy*, vol. 6 (1995), pp. 65–78. Some weaknesses of Putnam's thesis are explored in Michael Schudson, 'What if Civic Life Didn't Die?', *The American Prospect*, vol. 25 (March–April 1996), pp. 17–20.
[8] Claus Offe, 'After "The Great Transformation"', *CSD Bulletin*, vol. 5, no. 2 (Spring 1998), p. 12.

of markets – commodified economies tend to destroy the structures of civil society within which they are always and already embedded, and upon which they fundamentally depend for their reproduction. One example: adaptation to economic failure and change is never spontaneous or automatic, but depends upon a social infrastructure of assistance and incentives that enable adaptation to take place. Another example: market forces tend to spread into every nook and cranny of social life, thereby violating its plurality of voices and identities, which (as debates over good quality education and childcare facilities demonstrate) are themselves nevertheless indispensable to the functioning of market forces. And a final example: market forces display a definite blindness. They fail to recognize and to translate into price signals both present and future 'externalities', including the marginalization and exclusion of individuals, social groups and entire regions that are flung into the ranks of the disemployed. These 'market failures' – as Karl Polanyi famously pointed out in *The Origins of Our Time* (1945) – demonstrate that markets cannot create social order because the vital ingredients of social order cannot be produced by market interaction. Where there are no markets, civil societies find it impossible to survive. But the converse rule also applies: where there is no civil society, there can be no markets.

* * *

Phase two of the contemporary revival of interest in civil society and the state began during the 1970s in the central-eastern half of Europe. During this second phase, that region witnessed (as in Japan) the birth of public criticisms of despotic state power and the radical defence of civil society as an indispensable moment of a democratic political and social order. But in sharp contrast to the earlier Japanese breakthrough, the central-east European advocates of civil society parted company with Marxism. Among the pathbreaking efforts in this direction was a *samizdat* essay written by Jan Tesař, an unemployed Czech historian who specialized in analysing and comparing totalitarian regimes. He was among the initial signatories of Charter 77 and a co-founder of the Committee for the Defence of the Unjustly Prosecuted (VONS), and had recently been released from six years' imprisonment for 'subversive activity'.[9] According to Tesař, the various twentieth-century forms of totalitarian dictatorship (Stalinism, Nazism) were born of political instability and 'the undeveloped structure of civil society'. The origins of these party-dominated regimes show that democracy and totalitarianism are not opposites, for under crisis conditions, when the so-called 'broad masses' suddenly enter political life under conditions of a weakly developed civil society, totalitarian movements and parties feed parasitically upon such bowdlerized democratic slogans as 'all power to the soviets' and 'from the masses to the masses'. Totalitarian regimes are always born of 'a revolutionary crisis in society'. But the inverse rule also applies, argued Tesař. Not only is civil society the best antidote to the demagogy spawned by the mass ideologies and mass movements encouraged by the advance of the democratic ideal. The protracted struggle for civil society – not sudden revolution from above or below – is also the strongest weapon against totalitarian dictatorship once it is established. Civil society is the Achilles' heel of regimes such as Czechoslovakia: 'if the totalitarian systems, as a reversion to absolutism in the twentieth century, arise more easily in an environment where the structure of "civil society" is not sufficiently well formed, then the most reliable means of preventing their genesis is to encourage the development of that civil society'.

*   *   *

Democracy and Civil Society and *Civil Society and the State* fed upon the type of argument presented by Tesař. These books absorbed some of the 'spirit' of its iconoclasm, and at the same time tried to demonstrate its comparative strengths and limits – and the lessons it posed for countries, regions and peoples elsewhere in Europe, and beyond. The two volumes

[9] Jan Tesař, 'Totalitarian Dictatorships as a Phenomenon of the Twentieth Century and the Possibilities of Overcoming Them', originally prepared in typewritten form for the Biennale on Cultural Dissent in Venice, 1977, and translated and published in the *International Journal of Politics*, vol. 11, no. 1 (Spring 1981), pp. 85–100.

attempted to show the variety of overlapping and conflicting reasons why the old theme of civil society resurfaced in this 'forgotten half' of Europe. They suggested that within the one-party systems of countries such as Poland, Czechoslovakia and Yugoslavia, and especially within their democratic oppositions, the intellectual and practical interest in the subject of civil society was encouraged by the evident failure of reform communist attempts (as in the Prague Spring) to liberalize these systems from the top downwards. It was also fuelled by the conviction, widespread throughout the region, that these one-party systems could function only by thwarting this region's old traditions of civil society and, thus, by treating all individuals, groups and organizations as their property. During phase two of the theory of civil society, in other words, efforts were made to highlight the totalitarian character of Soviet-type systems. These systems were said to extinguish civil society by absorbing it fully into the bureaucratic structures of the Party-controlled state apparatus. The basic divisions between political and social power, public and private law, and state-sanctioned (dis-)information and publicly debated opinion were consequently seen to have been annihilated. So too were markets, in consequence of which these systems, despite the constant official boasting about planning, efficiency and 'the advantages of socialism', were marked by chronic planning failures, technical stagnation, waste and scarcity, and a staggering overdevelopment of an unproductive state apparatus of surveillance and control. In effect, these states were seen to place all citizens under permanent internment and surveillance – with public opposition of any kind being regarded as seditious.

Despite the state's permanent efforts to crush independent centres of power, the language of civil society functioned as an effective moral and political utopia in central and eastern Europe. Inspired by memories of besieged democratic traditions and convinced that the socialist project was exhausted, a variety of suppressed social interests, manifested in initiatives like KOR, Charta 77 and WiP, tried to protect themselves by forming alliances based on the principles of openness, solidarity and what Václav Havel famously called

'living in the truth'.[10] Such groups understood well that totalitarian state power could survive only if the (potential)
civil society was forced underground, shackled by apathy and
fear, and thereby reduced to 'the safety of the mousehole'
(György Konrád). The inverse of this point was also well
understood: whenever civil society gained in confidence, the
state's structural weaknesses and powerlessness would become evident. Civil society would swell rapidly from below.
It would feed upon whatever gains it could wrench from
state hands, which thereupon would likely suffer sprains
and paralysis. Elements of this dynamic became evident
in the Serbian events sketched in the opening of this book.
The dynamic first made its presence felt during the Polish
events of 1976–81, when downtrodden civilians, led by workers, struggled to establish a civil society (*spoleczenstwo
obywatelskie*) alongside and in opposition to a totalitarian state
(*panstwo*). Solidarność sought neither to form a political party
nor to 'capture' state power. It sought neither the restoration
of capitalism nor the withering away of the state. It rather
pursued a self-limiting 'evolutionist' strategy (which was
radicalized during 1981 into the idea of a 'self-governing republic' and modified several times under martial law). Its
ultimate goal was the cultivation of solidarity among a plurality of self-governing civil associations capable of pressur-
ing the state from without and enabling various groups to
attend peacefully to their non-state affairs.[11] Its moment of
triumph finally came in the autumn of 1989. In that year,
more or less 'velvet' revolutions broke out through the whole
region, forcing the Soviet Empire and its constituent regimes
into a state of collapse. The populations of the whole region
were then catapulted into the messy business of crafting political democracy, drawing new territorial boundaries, dealing with the national question, privatizing property and
marketizing social life, negotiating a 'return to Europe' and

[10] Václav Havel et al., *The Power of the Powerless*, ed. John Keane (London,
1985).
[11] See my interview (published using my nom-de-plume, Erica Blair) with
Adam Michnik, 'Towards a Civil Society: Hopes for Polish Society', *Times
Literary Supplement*, no. 4429 (19–25 February 1988), pp. 188, 198–99.

entry into the European Union – and doing so, wherever possible, with a measure of civility, patience and political wisdom.

* * *

During the past decade, which might be described as phase three of the renaissance of civil society, the 'footprint' of the term has spread well beyond the boundaries of Europe. Not only that, but the language of civil society, and its implied or explicit contrast with state institutions, has appeared in an extraordinary variety of intellectual contexts, with a variety of different meanings, and for a wide variety of purposes. It has, for instance, made a striking entry into scholarly examinations of the development of citizens' entitlements and duties within the European Union. The term has surfaced in the much-neglected discussion of children and their maltreatment; in the examination of controversies about the relationship between religion and politics; and in arguments for 'sub-politics' and 'ecological democracy' (Ulrich Beck). The same term is prominent in speculations about the ways in which the conclusion of the Cold War has unleashed new global tensions – for instance, between the potentially contradictory tasks of securing territorial state prerogatives based on legal-political criteria and the building of civil society associations based on normative pluralism. And some scholars are presently reflecting upon the possible emergence of a 'global' or 'international' civil society.[12]

During phase three, the language of civil society has also

---

[12] Examples include Elizabeth Meehan, *Citizenship and the European Community* (London, 1993), chapter 2; John O'Neill, *The Missing Child in Liberal Theory* (Toronto, Buffalo and London, 1994); David Hollenbach, 'The Contexts of The Political Role of Religion: Civil Society and Culture', *University of San Diego Law Review*, vol. 30, no. 4 (1993), pp. 877–901; Ulrich Beck, *Die Erfindung des Politischen* (Frankfurt am Main 1996), and 'World Risk Society? Ecological Questions in a Framework of Manufactured Uncertainties', *Theory, Culture and Society*, vol. 13, no 4 (1996), pp. 1–32; Mahmood Monshipouri, 'State Prerogatives, Civil Society, and Liberalization: The Paradoxes of the Late Twentieth Century in the Third World', *Ethics and International Affairs*, vol. 11 (1997), pp. 232–51; and Ariel Colonomos, 'La "Société civile globale": mirage ou oasis de l'international', unpublished paper (Paris, April 1998).

spread to an unprecedented variety of geographic contexts. In the Latin American area, for instance, discussions about civil society have featured in citizens' resistance to bureaucratic-authoritarian military regimes, in campaigns against terrorism and warlordism, and in proposed schemes (like Mercosur) of regional economic and political cooperation.[13] Scholarly studies of sub-Saharan Africa have emphasized how associational life – farmers' organizations in Kenya and Zimbabwe; lawyers' and journalists' associations in Ghana and Nigeria; mineworkers' unions in Zambia; Christian churches in Burundi and Kenya; Islamic brotherhoods in Senegal – are most likely to thrive in the presence of an effective state, and how, paradoxically, weak states can sometimes become stronger – more effective at promoting the accumulation and better distribution of wealth, and improving their own legitimacy and power potential – by allowing a good measure of pluralism in associational life.[14]

The term 'civil society' has also been used widely for political ends, as in South Africa, where groups like the South African National Civic Organization (SANCO) have helped to popularize talk of civil society in debates about the type of post-apartheid regime that is currently being born, or at least should be worked for. According to figures like Mzwanele Mayekiso, apartheid spawned the growth of networks of power-sensitive civil society groups, which sprang up in the densely packed communities of cardboard, plywood and zinc roofed huts, backyard repair shops, petty businesses ('spaza shops') and shacks-cum-hairdressing salons, and local bars ('shebeens'). These initially functioned as 'dual power' organizations designed to disrupt apartheid. According to Mayekiso, organs

[13] A good summary account of the degree to which the military regimes of Argentina, Brazil, Uruguay and Chile were supported or resisted by their civil societies is found in Alfred Stepan, 'State Power and the Strength of Civil Society in the Southern Cone of Latin America', in Peter B. Evans et al. (eds), *Bringing the State Back In* (New York, 1985), pp. 317–43.
[14] Michael Bratton, 'Beyond the State: Civil Society and Associational Life in Africa', *World Politics*, vol. 41 (April 1989), pp. 404–30; and Maxwell Owusu, 'Domesticating Democracy: Culture, Civil Society, and Constitutionalism in Africa', *Comparative Studies in Society and History*, vol. 39, no. 1 (January 1997), pp. 120–52.

such as the yard and street residents' committees, arts-and-craft organizations, burial societies and savings clubs must now strive to play the role of watchdogs on the ANC-led government, above all by ensuring that the low-wage, violence-ridden, police- and gang-harassed organs of civil society 'get greater resources and capacity to deliver goods in a manner free from the distortions of market power and state manipulation'.[15]

* * *

The language of civil society has also made a strong appearance for the first time in the east Asian region. The Japanese case has already been mentioned, but there have been many subsequent attempts to develop the theory of civil society, mainly in non-Gramscian ways. In Taiwan, the first systematic account of the dramatic history of press/state relations under Kuomintang one-party state rule has underlined the vital importance of the unintended, conflict-ridden emergence of a self-organizing civil society.[16] Important 'anthropological' controversies have broken out concerning how to translate the originally European term 'civil society' into local Asian languages. For instance, some Chinese scholars prefer the term 'citizen society' (*gongmin shehui*) or, like Taiwanese pro-opposition writer Nan Fang-So, 'popular society' (*minjian shehui*). Other writers prefer to speak of 'civilized society' (*wenming shehui*) or 'urban society' (*shimin shehui*).[17] And in the Korean peninsula, recent analyses have highlighted the contrasts between the totalitarian state of North Korea, whose rulers appear to have enjoyed absolute control over an obedient population, and South Korea, in which the long and bloody

[15] Mzwanele Mayekiso, 'The "Civics", Hope of the Townships', *Times Literary Supplement* no. 4748 (1 April 1994), p. 8. See also his *Township Politics. Civic Struggles for a New South Africa* (New York, 1996).

[16] Lihyun Lin, 'The Transformation of Press–State Relationships in Taiwan 1945–1995' (PhD dissertation, University of Westminster, London, 1997).

[17] Wang Shaoguang, 'Some Reflections on "Civil Society"', *Ershiyi Shiji* [Twenty-First Century], Hong Kong, no. 8 (December 1991), pp. 102–14. I am most grateful to Dr Lihyun Lin for her insightful remarks on this subject.

transition from the authoritarian rule of Syngman Rhee, top-
pled by the 19 April Student Uprising in 1960, has been driven
by the vigorous rebirth of civil society, whose roots are traceable to the struggle against Japanese colonization (1910–45)
and the massive peasant rebellions, called the Tonghak Upris-
ings, of the late nineteenth century.

The research by Hagen Koo and his colleagues is especially
interesting, and for several reasons.[18] Following the advice that
was repeatedly emphasized in *Democracy and Civil Society* and
Civil Society and the State, the South Korean case demonstrates
that there is no necessary zero-sum relationship between states
and civil societies. It shows, in other words, that a weak civil
society is not a logical correlate of a strong state, and (inversely)
that a strong, 'overdeveloped' state does not produce a docile
and quiescent society. The case of South Korea also under-
scores the utility of the civil society perspective in understanding the east Asian 'economic miracle'. Whereas conventional
views concentrate upon the developmental state and free-
market mechanisms as key explanations of the boom, Hagen
Koo and his colleagues concentrate as well on the dynamic,
sometimes unruly and conflict-ridden *social* underpinnings of
the state and market economy. Drawing explicitly on the interpretations offered in *Civil Society and the State*, they point
to the importance of social processes like the formation of
trade unions, the development of the *minjung* movement,
Confucianism and other moral and aesthetic reactions to
modernity. And by means of their civil society perspective
they point to an otherwise puzzling feature of South Korea's
rapid economic development – that despite their importance
in fuelling state-protected economic growth, large conglom-
erate business groups (*chaebŏl*) have been the focus of intense
popular resentment and opposition, which demonstrates that
South Korea is *not* an example of the so-called state capitalism with 'Asian values'.

*   *   *

Civil society perspectives have also surfaced in various guises

[18] See especially Hagen Koo (ed.), *State and Society in Contemporary Korea*
(Ithaca and London, 1993).

within the Muslim world, especially in the Arabic-speaking worlds of the al-Maghreb and al-Mashreq. Researchers specializing in the countries of the region have deployed the term to analyse the shifting contours and debates concerning state–civil society relations. The studies coordinated by Augustus Richard Norton are good examples.[19] The governments of this region are typically undemocratic – the world's highest concentration of despotisms is to be found in the zone stretching from Tangiers to Tehran – and perhaps it is to be expected that they have reacted to declining revenues, charges of malfeasance and misbehaviour, and growing social pressures by parroting – hypocritically – the rhetoric of civil society against Islamist groups and movements.

But of considerable importance is the growing interest in the concept of civil society *within* Islamic circles. In contexts in which it is a relatively simple matter to outlaw a party, but in which 'the Muslim state can no more shut down a mosque than a North American or European government can lock the doors of a church',[20] it is unsurprising that a growing number of Islamists speak the language of civil society with affection. They question the Eurocentric presumption that civil society, itself a European invention, cannot take root among Muslims. These Islamists insist that it is *not* true that Muslims are prone automatically to identify with segmentary communities guarded by an anonymous *Umma* in which men of faith, who 'do not seem to miss civil society too much', jostle for position through clientelist, cynical politics.[21] These same Islamists turn the tables on narrowly European definitions of civil society. They insist that secularism, conventionally thought to be a basic requirement of a civil society, effectively functions as an Orientalist ideology that protects despotic states bent on stifling the growth of civil societies within the Muslim

---

[19] See especially Augustus Richard Norton (ed.), *Civil Society in the Middle East* (Leiden, New York and Köln, 1994), vol. 1; and *Civil Society in the Middle East* (Leiden, New York and Köln, 1996).
[20] Augustus Richard Norton, 'Introduction', *Civil Society in the Middle East*, op. cit., vol. 2, p. 9.
[21] Ernest Gellner, *Encounters with Nationalism* (Oxford and Cambridge, Mass., 1994), p. 179.

world.[22]

This tendency is clearly evident in the recent speeches of Dr Mahathir bin Muhammad in Malaysia and President Khatami in Iran, where pressures are mounting for constitutional and political reform and economic and social reconstruction.[23] The same trend is especially evident in the Turkish context, where the emerging civil society is Islamist. Comprising networks of private schools, theatre groups, media organizations, clinics, mosques, computer firms and other businesses, civil society functions as the power base of a new middle class of university-educated groups, whose faith in God makes them strong critics of Kemalist 'secularism', mainly because it is regarded as *étatiste*, patronizing, potentially or actually violent, and riddled with such superstitions as the compulsory association of progress with the shaving of beards and the cultish worship of Atatürk. Continuing efforts by the armed forces to prevent further Islamicization of civil society and the state are bound to increase political tensions, ensuring that Turkey remains convulsed by two key forces: a military-authoritarian form of modernism aligned with the compulsory secularism instituted by Mustafa Kemal; and Muslim actors intent on developing and redefining civil society – pushing towards a post-secular civil society, structured by new codes of ethics and aesthetics and held together and institutionally protected by new post-secularist government policies in such fields as law, education, municipal administration, banking and foreign affairs.[24]

The pathbreaking scholarly reflections of Tunisian scholar

[22] See John Keane, 'The Limits of Secularism', *Times Literary Supplement*, 4945 (9 January 1998), pp. 12–13.

[23] The best recent studies are Anoushiravan Ehteshami, *After Khomeini: The Second Iranian Republic* (London and New York, 1995); and Farhad Kazemi, 'Civil Society and Iranian Politics', in Augustus Richard Norton (ed.), *Civil Society in the Middle East*, op. cit., vol. 2, pp. 119–52.

[24] Compare the analyses of Nilüfer Göle, *Musulmanes ets modernes: voile et civilisation en turquiee* (Paris, 1993), and her 'Toward an Autonomization of Politics and Civil Society in Turkey', in Metin Heper and Ahmet Evin (eds), *Politics in the Third Turkish Republic* (Boulder, Co., 1994), pp. 213–22; Serif Mardin, 'Civil Society and Islam', in John A. Hall, *Civil Society: Theory, History, Comparison* (Cambridge, 1995), pp. 278–300; and the intellectually stimu-

Rashid al-Ghannouchi on the subject of civil society have a good feel for this historic clash. Ghannouchi understands human beings as God's honoured vicegerents on earth. We have been gifted by the Creator with such attributes as language, body, mind, choice and will-power, and we are perforce expected to nurture these attributes. These God-given 'rights of man' are inalienable, but they also oblige human beings to exercise them prudently. 'God's rule' (*hukm-u-llah*) presupposes and requires 'people's rule' (*hukm-u-sha'ab*).[25] The human condition is caught between nature and God. It is sited in the realm of the between (*al-bayniyah*), which contains abundant spaces (*faraghat*) in which context-bound judgements (*ijtihad*) must be made by human beings and their representatives. Literal applications of the Quranic texts (*dhawahir an-nusus*) have important limits, argues Ghannouchi. The core of these texts (*al-Mokham*), covering such matters as the prohibition of stealing and murder, is not the proper subject of interpretation. Other strictures must however be 'translated', just as the followers of the Prophet who gathered in Aquaba did by pledging, by means of a contract (*bay'ah*), to establish an Islamic political community in Medina, founded upon the God-given principles of divine law and open consultation between governors and governed (*shura*). Just as the followers of the Prophet lived the relationship between *ad-dini* (the religious) and *as-siyasi* (the political), so Ghannouchi insists that the laws and institutions of a modern political community should nurture and honour the dignity of its citizens.

Ghannouchi here questions the rejection, by scholars such as Sy'd Q'utb, of political democracy as mere dross of a wholly corrupted world. In practice, he argues, the dignity of citizens is best nurtured by institutionalizing the democratic principle of popular sovereignty through such mechanisms as periodic elections, the separation of powers, equality before the law, a

---

lating note by Abdelwahab El-Affendi, 'From Istanbul with Love . . . and Fear: The Trials and Tribulations of Turkish "Secularism"', *Muslim Politics Report* (Council on Foreign Relations, Washington, DC, June–July 1997), pp. 3–4.
[25] Rashid al-Ghannouchi, *Ad-Dini was-Siyasi Fil-Islam* [The Religious and the Political in Islam], a lecture delivered to the Cardiff Islamic Society, Cardiff (January 1997).

multiparty system, freedom of expression, and the right of the majority to rule and of the minority publicly to oppose that rule.[26] But Ghannouchi goes further than appealing to Muslims and others to respect and to use the institutions of modern political democracy – even to accept with good grace defeat by their opponents in free elections. He insists that Muslims must also use their human capacities for reason (*'aql*) and *ijtihad* and work to create, renew and nurture civil society institutions (*al-mujtama' al-ahli*).[27] Ghannouchi is aware that Arab 'secularists' today misuse the term, in countries such as Egypt and Tunisia, as a weapon with which to denigrate and politically violate their Islamist opponents.[28] He is perhaps less aware of having used the term 'civil society' in two conflicting ways. Sometimes the term 'civil society' (*al-ahli*) is reserved for an Islamic political community whose powers are restricted by *Shari'ah*, in which case Muslims established a civil state, more than fourteen centuries ago, in Medina (pre-

---

[26] Rashid al-Ghannouchi, *Al-Hurriyat Al-'Ammah Fiddawlah Al-Islamiyah* (Beirut, 1993), forthcoming in English translation as *Public Liberties in the Islamic State*.

[27] Sometimes Ghannouchi uses the term *al-mujtama' al-ahli* to refer to a political order which straddles the conventional division between traditional and modern societies, in that it comprises such associations as trade unions, the souk, the mosque, schools and households. The Arabic word *al-ahl* conveys several meanings, including inhabitants, family, wife, husband, children, relatives and people. More frequently, Ghannouchi, like other Islamists, especially in Egypt, prefers instead to speak of civil society using the term *al-mujtama' al-madani*, which comprises specifically modern institutions, such as trade unions, political parties, student organizations and professional associations. *Madina* is the word for city. *Madani* (from *madan*, to civilize or to refine, as contrasted with *al-sahara*, the desert, with its connotations of savagery, the unpolished and unrefined) has several meanings, including city-dwelling, urban, civilized and polished. I am most grateful to Rafik Bouchlaka and Azzam Tamimi, doctoral research students at the Centre for the Study of Democracy, for helpful comments on this section.

[28] Rashid al-Ghannouchi, 'Tunisia: The Islamic Movement and Civil Society', an unpublished paper presented at Pretoria University, South Africa (August 1994). See also his essay (in Arabic), 'Westernisation and the Necessity of Dictatorship', originally published in Elghurabaā, vol. 6, no. 6 (September 1980), reprinted in Rashid al-Ghannouchi, *Maquālāt* (Paris, 1984), pp. 167–70.

viously called Yathreb). More often, the term 'civil society' (*al-madani*) is used to refer to a particular kind of modern, non-violent political order (*al-dawla*) in which social actors are employers of the political authorities, whose mission is to service the needs of society. It is principally in the latter sense that he insists that the secularist dictatorships of the al-Maghreb and al-Mashreq regions are actually hostile to their fledgling civil societies, which are best nurtured and protected by renewing religious faith and its corresponding morality of power sharing, including 'social solidarity, civil liberties, human rights . . . freedom of the press, and liberty for mosques and Islamic activities'.[29] These emergent *post-secular* civil societies not only pose a challenge to political despotism (*al-tasallot*). They also promise the transition from the 'natural condition' of power and necessity towards the rule of law, or to what Ghannouchi calls the legitimacy of popular choice. Tradition-bound tribal societies and contemporary despotisms are examples of natural communities that resemble communities of ants and bees, in which belonging is involuntary, government is instinctive, and laws tend to be unchangeable. A civil society, by contrast, is a community of actors whose legally inscribed patterns of association are voluntary, which means that its members are equipped with the power to reinterpret and to transform the social and political structures within which they interact.

[29] Rachid Ghannouchi, 'The Participation of Islamists in a Non-Islamic Government', in Azzam Tamimi (ed.), *Power-Sharing Islam?* (London, 1993), p. 56.

Distinctions

All these developments suggest that the language of civil society is now more widely used than ever before in the history of modern times, including the century of its birth and maturation (1750–1850).[1] The 'emigration' of the term from Europe is in itself an impressive achievement, especially when it is considered that the subject has entered into broader public discourse. Not only has the term become familiar within circles of academics and journalists. Non-governmental organizations and political actors of various persuasions – from the Prime Minister of the Islamic Republic of Iran to the President of the Czech Republic – are also inclined to speak the language of civil society. So striking is the popularization of the term that it could even be said that the language of civil society is currently undergoing a vertical and horizontal 'globalization'. Individuals, groups, organizations in every corner of the earth now speak its language. Some even speak of an emergent 'global civil society'.

This global extension of the concept is an entirely novel development, which is arguably having both positive and negative practical effects. On the positive side, the worldwide expansion of the language of civil society is evidently bound

[1] See my 'Despotism and Democracy: The Origins and Development of the Distinction Between Civil Society and the State 1750–1850', in John Keane (ed.), *Civil Society and the State: New European Perspectives* (London and New York, 1988) [hereafter cited as *Civil Society and the State*], pp. 35–71.

up with the dramatic growth, especially during the second half of this century, of non-governmental civic organizations operating at the international level; whereas there were just over 100 such bodies in 1900, there are today more than 10,000, and their estimated number continues to rise quickly. The global talk of civil society may even signal the first step in the long-term emergence of common frameworks of meaning underneath and across state boundaries – a language that resonates with, and practically reinforces, such trends as the rebirth of international humanitarian law prohibiting genocide, and the growth of a shared (if diffuse) sense within non-governmental organizations and publics at large that civilians have obligations to other civilians living beyond their borders simply because they are civilians. It is doubtful that the spreading talk of civil society is just talk. The symbol of 'civil society' possesses its own causal power in the double meaning of the French verb *causer*: talking by means of symbolic signifiers *and* precipitating an effect.

But which effect? There are in reality many different effects upon those who speak warmly of civil society, including their emphasis on the need to reduce violence in human affairs and the heightened common sense of the importance of division and diversity within the body politic – and the suspicion of what I have called the Myth of Collective Harmony, with its dangerous belief in the possibility of a world without division and conflict, its disgust for the political, its quest for actors' authenticity and mutual recognition of Truth, and its fantasy of abolishing state institutions based on representatives, spokespersons, delegates, mandate-holders. These 'civil' sentiments are presently feeding the worldwide popularity of the language of civil society. Its popularity is feeding in turn upon the noticeable loss of energy and even outright exhaustion – for the time being – of the vision of the territorial state as the bearer of an ethical project bent on reshaping and reordering the identity of its inhabitants. There have been various twentieth-century versions of this state-centred vision – Third World Liberation, the Keynesian welfare state, fascism, socialism, nationalism, modernization and so on – but after a century of practical experimentation with their respective ideals

it appears that their moon has waned. Armed territorial states
are commonly seen as chief culprits in the awful bloodshed
and bullying that have marked the long century of violence
that is now drawing to a close. There is also spreading awareness of the normative and technical *limits* of what territorial
states can or should try to achieve for their populations in
such matters as business investment, artistic innovation and
urban regeneration.

So we see the waxing moon of civil society and the begin-
nings of a worldwide search for new equilibriums between
state and non-state institutions. It is doubtful that this search
is a simple, unmediated reflection of the recent emergence of
global economic forces, the 'globalization' of foreign trade and
direct investment, and the growing mismatch between the
scale of markets and the territorially bound state. The notion
that states were once 'sovereign' in economic matters is questionable. So too is the double presumption that capitalist states
were once geopolitically autonomous and economic growth
once took place without international regulatory institutions.
But there can be no doubt that certain new trends – the
internationalization of telecommunications, the domination
of international accounting practice by a handful of big Anglo-
American firms, the influence of the 'econocrats' of major international organizations like the IMF – are having deeply
unsettling effects upon territorial states, which are not so much
retreating as redirecting their priorities in the field of economic governance towards the interests of large corporations
and the wealthier social classes.[2]

The warm reference to civil society by the Prime Minister of
Malaysia, cited at the beginning of this book, can be under-

---

[2] Compare Susan Strange, *The Retreat of the State: The Diffusion of Power in
the World Economy* (Cambridge and New York, 1996) and Paul Hirst, *From
Statism to Pluralism* (London, 1997), part 3. The one-sided argument that
the globalization of the term 'civil society' is embedded in 'the logic of
liberal capitalist society and the capitalist global division of labour' is put
directly by David L. Blaney and Mustapha Kamal Pasha, 'Civil Society and
Democracy in the Third World: Ambiguities and Historical Possibilities',
Studies in Comparative International Development, vol. 28, no. 1 (Spring 1993),
pp. 3–24.

stood in this way. But talk of civil society is not – and in modern times never has been – simply 'bourgeois ideology'. There are other and bigger causes. The current 'globalization' of the language of civil society is overdetermined, for instance, by the dysfunctions resulting from 'the overreach of the state' (Chandhoke), and by the spreading conviction that only civil societies can do certain things, or perform certain functions best. It is also overdetermined by the sharpened awareness that various twentieth-century states have inflicted dastardly deeds upon their subjects, and that this must never be allowed to happen again. The combined effect of these different overlapping forces is to foster the search for new compromises between states and societies. There are plenty of contemporary examples, including the controversies about how to rebuild 'failed states' and the pathbreaking efforts to build supranational states. So too are neo-liberal and post-social democratic or 'New Labour' attempts to 'reinvent government' (making government steer more and row less by doing everything 'faster, smarter, cheaper, better')[3] and efforts to fashion 'welfare-to-work' strategies by replacing universalist social policies with targeted state support for certain social groups. Other examples include efforts to craft Islamic republics; unprecedented attempts to construct and consolidate democratic institutions in post-communist countries; and the contemporary Chinese-style pursuit of *perestroika* without *glasnost*. In each of these experiments in the political art of reshaping state forms and setting new limits upon the scope and power of state institutions, the topic of civil society plays a part, even if only as an implied alternative. In each case, a civil society, or a *more civil* civil society is considered to be an important political objective. Social institutions such as markets, public spheres and voluntary associations that are outside the direct control of the state are considered a good thing. Grand fictions about the primacy of state institutions are thus laid to rest. In their place emerge new controversies about the possible types of compromise between state and civilian

[3] See Guy Peters, *Future of Governing: Four Emerging Models* (London, 1997). Compare the parallel arguments, in the quite different context of India, of Neera Chandhoke, *State and Civil Society: Explorations in Political Theory* (New Delhi, 1995).

institutions, and about the nature, performance and limits of civil society institutions themselves.

*   *   *

The worldwide presumption that greater toleration of social differences capable of non-violent political representation is a desirable objective is a mixed blessing for the increasingly polysemic signifier 'civil society'. Its burgeoning popularity accelerates the accumulation of inherited ambiguities, new confusions and outright contradictions. For this reason alone, the expanding talk of civil society is not immune to muddle and delirium. There are even signs that the meanings of the term 'civil society' are multiplying to the point where, like a catchy advertising slogan, it risks imploding through overuse. There certainly is growing agreement about the importance of civil society, but there is also growing disagreement about its exact meaning. Some commentators even seem to want to confuse the subject in order to complain about the 'elusiveness' of the concept of civil society.[4] What continues to be lacking – little has changed in this respect since the publication of my original two volumes – is clarity about the plethora of conflicting usages of the state–civil society schema. *Civil Society and the State* distinguished among three crisscrossing but different ways of wielding the distinction, and there is no good reason for withdrawing this typology, despite the passage of time. Although these three approaches usually overlap and complement each other, they also tend to produce divergent types of claim and should therefore be distinguished. In the following few sections, the three approaches are illustrated by way of new research published during the past decade. It will become evident that some writers utilize the term 'civil society' to analyse and interpret the empirical contours of past, present or emergent relationships between social and political forces and institutions. It will be shown that others see the term mainly in 'pragmatic' terms, as a guide in formulating a social and political strategy or action programme; and that still others view the distinction normatively – that is, to high-

[4] An example is Philip Resnick, *Twenty-First Century Democracy* (Kingston and Montréal, 1997), chapter 7.

light the ethical superiority of a politically guaranteed civil
society compared with other types of regime.

* * *

The concept of civil society is today often used as an *idealtyp*
to describe, explain, clarify and understand the contours of a
given slice of complex reality. The immediate or avowed aim
of such *empirical-analytic interpretations* of civil society is not
to recommend courses of political action or to form normative judgements. Rather, the language of civil society is used
to develop an explanatory understanding of a complex sociopolitical reality by means of theoretical distinctions, empirical
research and informed judgements about its origins, patterns
of development and (unintended) consequences. Although
empirical-analytic interpretations of civil society usually alter
perceptions of what is or is not significant within any given
reality, the term is mainly used for observational purposes:
that is, to describe that reality, or criticize prevailing descriptions of it, in order better to clarify what is otherwise a potentially confusing and disorientating reality.

The clarificatory effects of the descriptive language of civil
society are evident in the scholarly controversy sparked by
Liu Zhiguang and Wang Suli, Chinese co-authors of one of
the first essays published on the mainland to urge the creation
of a civil society (*gongmin shehui*) within a regime that had
fed hitherto upon a deep-seated culture of 'dependency on
the state'.[5] According to Liu and Wang, China lacks a strong
democratic tradition. Right down to the end of the Qing dynasty, the population regarded itself as 'subjects' (*chenmin*),
and even after the 1911 Revolution, when 'the people' (*renmin*)
and 'citizens' (*gongmin*) were enshrined, the living tradition of
despotism was not defeated. In traditional Confucian thought,
they argued, the abstract concept of 'society', separate from

[5] Liu Zhiguang and Wang Suli, 'From "Mass Society" to "Civil Society"',
Xinhua wenzhai [New China Digest] (Beijing), vol. 11, no. 119 (1988), p. 9.
I am most grateful to my CSD colleague Dr Harriet Evans for help in trans-
lating and interpreting this essay. Further discussion of the Chinese case is
found in Shu-Yun Ma, 'The Chinese Discourse on Civil Society', *The China
Quarterly*, no. 137 (March 1994), pp. 180–93.

individual existences, went unacknowledged. The neologism *shehui* (the term for 'communal religious meetings' in the Song dynasty) had to be borrowed from the Japanese, who had derived it in turn from the European meaning of 'society' as an ensemble of voluntary associations somehow counterposed to the hierarchy, majesty and power of governmental and state institutions. Liu and Wang implied that although Chinese political culture has had a long tradition of protest against injustice and, correspondingly, of recognizing differences between people acting within and outside governmental circles, the meanings of terms like *guan* (official), *gong* (public) and *si* (private) remained both indistinct and ambiguous. Old habits have remained, they noted. China not only bears the birthmarks of its traditional system of autocratic monarchy, which demanded absolute obedience from its subjects, and a patriarchal clan system, which demanded the same of its sons and daughters. China today suffers the effects of a centralizing socialist state. It is describable as a 'mass society' (*qunzhong shehui*), a term whose classical roots connote a multitude of subordinate people who resemble a group of animals who do not know the meaning of the idea of a 'free person' (*ziyou min*) whose civil entitlements are protected by legal checks upon the exercise of power.

Liu and Wang came close to saying that the construction of a civil society in China required nothing less than a great leap forwards – not in the Maoist sense, but rather towards originally modern European standards of civility, the rule of law and publicly accountable power. The daunting challenge seemed to be taken up a year later by the Tiananmen events of 1989, the outbreak and brutal suppression of which have nevertheless triggered a rich scholarly controversy about whether those events represented a temporary victory of the project of westernization – something like the spreading of the language of civil society from West to East – or whether they are better understood as an episode in a very much older, indigenous Chinese project of publicly contesting illegitimate power. The two interpretations are, of course, not necessarily antithetical, and indeed among the more striking features of the scholarly discussion of civil society in the Chinese context is the way in which it has effected a reconsideration of the history of Chinese political thinking and political culture.

Against the stereotypical view of China as a species of Asiatic despotism, particular research emphasis has been given to the argument that protest against state power, especially efforts to shame leaders into reforming their ways, have old roots, traceable to the rhetoric of remonstrance and retribution and the calls for freedom of speech, civil rights and fair elections evident in the May Fourth Movement of 1919 and the subsequent May Fourth-style demonstrations of the 1920s, 1930s and 1940s.[6] Emphasis has also been placed upon the deeply rooted tendency towards social self-organization and defences of group autonomy (*tuanti zidong*) against the invasions of officials and warlords. It is argued that, just as from the mid-eighteenth century European cities like Paris and London witnessed the growth of circles, clubs and coffeehouses that produced a steady stream of independent commentary about politics, so in Beijing by the 1920s there existed a dense mosaic of locality inns (*huiquan*), locality clubs (*tongxianghui*), bathhouses, restaurants, teahouses, brothels, craft and merchant guilds, temples, pavilions and public parks, all of which functioned partly as public spheres of (potential) controversy about power.[7]

Research emphasis has also been placed, finally, on the myriad of self-regulating segmented associations that developed in late imperial China. Such enquiry is an important challenge to the pervasive western habit of describing 'China' as a changeless, despotic entity, although to characterize these associations as a 'distinct premodern civil society'[8] is to commit a contradiction in terms – civil societies are by definition modern. But still the descriptive claim stands: in the aftermath of the Taiping Rebellion (1851–64) segmentary groups

---

[6] Dorothy J. Solinger, 'Democracy with Chinese Characteristics', *World Policy Journal* (Fall 1989), pp. 621–32, especially pp. 625–6.

[7] David Strand, 'Protest in Beijing: Civil Society and Public Sphere in China', *Problems of Communism*, vol. 34 (May–June 1990), pp. 4–5.

[8] Mayfair Mei-hui Yang, 'Between State and Society: The Construction of Corporateness in a Chinese Socialist Factory', *Australian Journal of Chinese Affairs* (July 1989), p. 35.

Distinctions

like guilds, surname and neighbourhood associations, and religious groupings such as temple societies, deity cults, secret societies and monasteries all grew in strength and influence. So too did the so-called professional associations (*fatuan*) of chambers of commerce, bankers' and lawyers' circles and other groupings in many cities and towns.[9] Through these various associations, local elites developed an interest in 'self-help' (*zizhu*); assumed some measure of control over such tasks as trade and commerce, poor relief, water conservation and maintaining order; and articulated criticisms of the government's domestic and foreign policies. These groups functioned as arms of state power and, at the same time, as media for crystallizing social interests. In other words, these groups can be seen as proto-civil associations, even though their overall identity and day-to-day functioning as organs of self-rule (*zizhi*) normally remained dependent upon official rule (*guanzhi*) organized by state officials equipped with the power to confer or withdraw their accreditation, and the power to frustrate and check their potential autonomy, ultimately through the use of police and army violence.

Seen against the backdrop of the century-long rise of proto-civil associations and the more recent impact of the post-Mao market reforms, the Tiananmen events, even allowing for their exceptionally dramatic and violent ending, look less an exception inspired by 'westernization' and more consistent with an older, but distinctively modern Chinese tradition of conflict between the principles of self-rule and official diktat. This tradition is not necessarily democratic, for as Wang Shaoguang has reminded us, emergent civil societies are usually riven by inequalities and conflicts that can lead to various outcomes, of which democracy is but one.[10] Yet it might still be possible to draw from the historical evidence summarized above the broad inference that contemporary China is today feeling the pow-

---

[9] See the studies of Mary Rankin, *Elite Activism and Political Transformation in China* (Stanford, 1986); Mark Elvin and G.W. Skinner (eds), *The Chinese Society Between Two Worlds* (Stanford, 1974); and Susan Mann, *Local Merchants and the Chinese Bureaucracy, 1750–1950* (Stanford, 1987).
[10] Wang Shaoguang, 'Some Reflections on "Civil Society"', *Ershiyi Shiji* [Twenty-First Century], Hong Kong, no. 8 (December 1991), pp. 102–14.

erful pinch of the past, in that significant parts of its population are experiencing the slow but irreversible breakdown of
totalitarian rule, which is arguably an exceptional episode of
modern Chinese history. Symptomatic of this breakdown is
the open emergence of some independent social initiatives,
such as unofficial women's and workers' organizations, the
growth of a myriad of hybrid 'social organizations' (*shehui
tuanti*) on the edges of state power, and a growing number of
state-dominated 'mass organizations' (*qunzhong zuzhi*), whose
members are working from inside the cages of the party-state
to reshape its structures and functions.[11]

*   *   *

The language of civil society can also be used for the purposes
of calculating political strategies of achieving a predefined or
assumed political good. In contrast to empirical-analytic-
interpretative approaches, which are concerned with such intellectual tasks as naming, categorizing, observing, theorizing,
comparing and understanding a complex reality of institutionally structured action, *strategic usages* of the distinction between civil society and the state have an eye for defining what
must or must not be done so as to reach a given political goal.
The term 'civil society' is bound up with efforts to calculate
the tactical *means* of achieving or preserving certain ends.

Although there is a variety of possible strategic usages of
the modern term 'civil society', the original version is traceable to the last quarter of the eighteenth century – to recommendations, like Thomas Paine's revolutionary pamphlet
Common Sense, about how best to contest despotic power by
establishing the earthworks of civil society.[12] In recent dec-

---

[11] See the various analyses of X.L. Ding, 'Institutional Amphibiousness and
the Transition from Communism: The Case of China', *British Journal of
Political Science*, vol. 24 (1994), pp. 293–318; He Baogang, 'The Dual Roles
of Semi-Civil Society in Chinese Democracy', *Institute of Development Studies Discussion Paper*, no. 327 (August 1993); and Gordon White et al., *In
Search of Civil Society: Market Reform and Social Change in Contemporary
China* (Oxford, 1996).

[12] Paine's strategic understanding of 'society' and 'government' is analysed
in my *Tom Paine: A Political Life* (London and New York, 1995), pp. 104–29.

ades, and especially during phase one of the renewed talk of civil society, the term has been mobilized for tactical ends mainly by writers and activists who stand within the Gramscian tradition. There are numerous problems with their approach – several of the key ones are highlighted above, as well as in the first two volumes in this trilogy – which implies the need for *post-Gramscian*, or even *non-Gramscian*, tactical usages of the state–civil society distinction.

My proposed theory of the politics of retreat is an example of the latter.[13] It takes issue with the dominant preoccupation within modern political philosophy to concentrate either upon the process of capturing and maintaining the key resources of power (examples include Machiavelli's *Il principe* or Carl Schmitt's *Die Diktatur*); or upon the process of limiting, controlling and apportioning state power (an example of which is *The Federalist*, drafted by James Madison and others). Although the two standpoints are indispensable to theoretical analyses of power, they are in fact complementary, since each presumes that the lust for political power is both polymorphous and universal. Edmund Burke expressed this conventional point succinctly in *A Letter to a Member of the National Assembly*: 'Those who have been once intoxicated with power, and have derived any kind of emolument from it, even though but for one year, can never willingly abandon it.'[14] Thomas Hobbes's *Leviathan* put the same point more pithily:

> Kings, whose power is greatest, turn their endeavours to the assuring it at home by Lawes, or abroad by Wars: and when that is done, there succeedeth a new desire; in some, of Fame from new Conquest; in others, of ease and sensuall pleasure; in others, of admiration, or being flattered for excellence in some art, or other ability of the mind.[15]

[13] John Keane, 'The Politics of Retreat', *The Political Quarterly*, vol. 61, no. 3 (July–September 1990), pp. 340–52.
[14] Edmund Burke, 'A Letter to a Member of the National Assembly, in Answer to Some Objections to His Book on French Affairs', in *The Works of The Right Honourable Edmund Burke* (London, 1859), vol. 4, p. 11.
[15] Thomas Hobbes, *Leviathan, or The Matter, Forme, & Power of a Commonwealth Ecclesiasticall and Civil* (London, 1651 [1968]), part 1, chapter 11.

What these dominant modern perspectives on power have failed systematically to analyse are instances of *retreat from power*. Consider the recent crop of political leaders whose chief function is to contribute to the *dismantling* of a despotic political system. Latin American analysts long ago recognized the importance of 'state-led liberalization from above',[16] but in European political analyses this process has rarely been discussed, despite a succession of political figures skilled in the tasks of dismantling power: Adolfo Suarez, who forced through a democratic constitution upon becoming Spanish prime minister after Franco's death; János Kádár, who survived the fall of Khrushchev and eventually helped prepare the way for market reforms and a multiparty system in Hungary; Alexander Dubček, the symbol of reform communism in the 1960s and a protagonist of the 1989 velvet revolution in Czechoslovakia; Constantine Karamanlis, who with high-ranking military support facilitated the dismantling of the 'regime of the colonels' in Greece; Wojciech Jaruzelski, who eventually colluded with the formation of the first Solidarność-led government in Poland; Milan Kučan, the protagonist of constitutional reform in Slovenia; and Mikhail Gorbachev, who walked in the footsteps of Nikita Khrushchev, the first leader to attempt to dismantle the Soviet system from above.

These politicians should not be thought of as strong-willed, charismatic and (potentially) iron-fisted figures – like Woodrow Wilson, Mussolini, Roosevelt, Churchill, Stalin, Hitler, Adenauer, de Gaulle, Kohl, Mitterrand, Thatcher and others before them – who devote their lives to preserving or expanding their state's integrity at home and abroad. Suarez, Gorbachev, Karamanlis and others represent a different species of political animal. They are best understood as politicians of retreat. Although schooled in the arts of conventional politics – politicians of retreat always begin their careers in the corridors and committee rooms of state power – they are not driven by lust for power or visions of grand victories

[16] Guillermo O'Donnell et al., *Transitions from Authoritarian Rule* (Baltimore and London, 1986).

through conquest. They are instead skilled practitioners of the difficult art of unscrewing the lids of despotism and enabling the growth of civil society, mainly by forging new compromises between state actors and their subjects, and by withdrawing and retreating from unworkable positions.

Some politicians of retreat learn this art retrospectively, when the process of dismantling in which they are embroiled has already begun. This is unsurprising, since the art of retreat, as von Clausewitz explained in his *Vom Kriege*,[17] is the most difficult of all political skills to learn. It requires an ability to know the difference between foolishness and magnanimity. It entails knowing when and how to blow the whistle on (potential) opponents, to abandon untenable positions and to slip through the loopholes of retreat. It sometimes necessitates surrendering the middle ground and it always requires mettle, acumen, nerve, toughness and patience. The politics of retreat is naturally a delicate and dangerous process. Its protagonists are trapped constantly in the quicksands of politics. They risk their careers and lives at every step, and they are always surrounded by enemies lurking in the shadowy corners of state power. Ingratitude of many of their rivals and subjects is their ultimate fate. The wisest politicians of retreat know from the outset that they must be ruined for the good of others.

Their legitimacy problem stems partly from the fact that, unlike early modern enlightened bureaucrat reformers who aimed to strengthen society without initiating political reforms, politicians of retreat work for the disintegration of the existing despotic regime, thereby threatening certain individuals and groups whose power base lies within this system. The politicians of retreat also suffer unpopularity because they normally insist on doing without certain privileges or customary routines. They help dramatically to widen the political spectrum, but this is not to everyone's liking. Their actions breed the uncertainty and confusion typical of a 'post-prison psychosis' (Havel). And politicians of retreat rarely offer im-

---

[17] Karl Philipp Gottlieb von Clausewitz, 'Vom Kriege', in *Hinterlassene Werke über Krieg und Kriegführung* (Berlin, 1832–4), books 1–3.

mediate positive benefits to their supporters. They tend to speak the language of future gains, and they know one thing best: that despotic regimes can die of swallowing their own lies and arrogance, and that fear and demoralization cannot govern for ever.

The politicians of retreat also lead a tenuous and unpopular – and usually short – existence because their actions often have the unintended consequence of fostering the growth of *social* power groups acting at a distance from the despotic state which they help to dismantle. In helping to disarm the Leviathan, the politicians of retreat encourage the growth of a self-organizing civil society, whose chattering, conflicts and rebellions unnerve them. They learn too slowly that effective government requires winning the trust of citizens, and that this involves more than dismantling or scheming, rapacity, peacockery and shouting orders. For all these reasons, but especially because they play the role of midwives of civil society, the politicians of retreat typically sow the seeds of their own downfall. In the end, they usually prove no match for the political and social forces which they help to unleash. They become victims of their own success. Some politicians of retreat suffer bitter disappointment when their reforms prove to be stillborn. Others have the cold comfort of knowing that their experiments with the status quo lead to consolidated reforms. Some politicians of retreat find that their experiments in reform breed revolutions.

* * *

Others have used the category of civil society to analyse, in different but complementary ways, the factors that enable strategies of political dismantling to succeed. It is obvious (as *Democracy and Civil Society* emphasized) that the birth or rebirth of civil society is an utterly difficult and ambiguous process. Not only do regimes never end their day by taking two capsules of liberalism, only to wake up next morning to find that they have been democratized, and that their civil societies are thriving. The birth or rebirth of civil society is always riddled with dangers, for it gives freedom to despots and democrats alike. During the politics of retreat, civil society can degenerate into a battlefield in which, thanks to the existence of certain civil liberties, foxes enjoy the freedom to hunt down chickens. The growth of democracy, the pluralization of power within a civil society protected and encouraged by a strong framework of accountable state institutions, is only one particular form of state–civil society relationship. Under what conditions, it can then be asked, is democracy in this sense most likely to emerge, and to survive?

The single most convincing response to this question is Juan Linz and Alfred Stepan's pathbreaking comparative study of the defeat of various forms of political despotism in southern Europe, South America and post-communist Europe. Their *Problems of Democratic Transition and Consolidation* boldly formulates a theory of the preconditions of a successful transition towards democracy and the subsequent conditions that enable the consolidation of a democratic regime.[18] Linz and Stepan emphasize that democratization is a tender plant. Democracy has no metahistorical guarantees. It is certainly not written into the nature of things. Employing a variety of methods – typological, content and survey analyses; neo-institutional and path-dependent approaches; game theory; and extensive interviews with key actors – they show that most episodes of political change away from once-stable non-democratic regimes never result in 'completed democratic transitions'. Fewer still become what they call 'consolidated democracies'. And even some consolidated democracies can and do break down.

From their democratic perspective, this fragility of the democratization process is important to understand and to explain. They acknowledge the critical importance of the character – totalitarian; post-totalitarian; authoritarian; or sultanistic – of the regime that predated the attempted democratic transition, which leads them to argue for a modified 'path-dependent' approach in understanding the process of democratization. Linz and Stepan also acknowledge the unpredictable effects of contingencies like prudent leadership

---

[18] Juan J. Linz and Alfred Stepan, *Problems of Democratic Transition and Consolidation: Southern Europe, South America, and Post-Communist Europe* (Baltimore and London, 1996), especially part 1.

(which is the focus of my politics of retreat thesis). They emphasize as well variables like timing and the element of surprise – 'the specificities of history' – and they also insist that the existence of a 'sovereign state' is an essential prerequisite for democracy. They argue – here they are explicitly critical of a 'classic' work by Guillermo O'Donnell, Philippe Schmitter and Laurence Whitehead, *Transitions from Authoritarian Rule* (1986) – that in many countries the crisis of the non-democratic *ancien régime* is also intermixed with profound political differences about what should actually count as the polity or political community, and which *demos* or *demoi* should be members of that political community. When there are profound differences both about the territorial boundaries of the political community's state and about who has the right to be included as citizens of that state, there is what they call a problem of 'stateness'. Where it exists, the 'stateness' problem is not easily solved, exactly because every attempted transition to a consolidated democracy faces a conundrum. Here is the problem: unless an organization with state-like attributes exists in a territory, a government, not even one which is 'democratically elected', cannot effectively exercise its claim to the monopoly of the legitimate use of force in the territory, cannot collect taxes (and thus provide any public services), and cannot secure a judicial system. And yet this indispensable political prerequisite of democratic government normally cannot be decided democratically. The democratic process *presupposes* the rightfulness of the political unit itself. If the political unit is not from the outset considered legitimate by the population which votes, then democratic procedures cannot make it legitimate. Agreements about stateness are logically prior to the creation of democratic institutions.

Linz and Stepan proceed from these arguments to specify the preconditions of the successful consolidation of democracy. They point to five variables that must be in place within any context in order for democratic institutions to survive, and even to thrive. The persistence through time of a stable territorial state with an effective bureaucracy has already been mentioned (although a point that is neglected here is whether

or not Linz and Stepan's approach can adequately compre-
hend the current struggle to establish and to consolidate democratic institutions within 'pillared', post-territorial state
institutions, such as those of the emerging European Union).[19]
Secondly, democratic consolidation in their view also requires
all significant actors, especially governments and state institutions, to respect and to uphold the rule of law. A spirit of
constitutionalism requires more than rule by majoritarianism,
they insist. It also entails a relatively strong consensus about
the constitution, an independent judicial system, a clear sense
of the hierarchy of laws, a strong legal culture, and a commitment to not changing the laws unless so favoured by a large
majority of voters.

The consolidation of democracy also necessitates, thirdly, 'a
free and lively civil society'. Linz and Stepan argue against
those politicians and party-supporting intellectuals who insist
that civil society, having played its historic role in contesting
political despotism, should be *demobilized* so as to allow for
the development of stable democratic government. 'A robust
civil society', they comment, has 'the capacity to generate
political alternatives and to monitor government and state'. It
can help 'transitions get started, help resist reversals, help push
transitions to their completion, help consolidate, and help
deepen democracy. At all stages of the democratization process,' they write, 'a lively and independent civil society is in-
valuable.' Linz and Stepan go on to conclude that the vital
role played by civil society in securing democracy must in
turn be backed up by the existence of two other, closely related sets of institutions. A democratically organized civil society requires a 'political society': that is, mechanisms such as
political parties and interparty alliances, elections and elec-
toral rules, political leaders and legislatures, through which
the citizens of a civil society constitute themselves as citizens
and select and monitor democratically elected governments.
Linz and Stepan also add a fifth and final condition of democratic consolidation: an institutionalized 'economic society',

[19] See the contrasting type of analysis presented by Ulrich Preuss, 'Problems of a Concept of European Citizenship', *European Law Journal*, vol. 1
(November 1995), pp. 267–81.

by which they do not mean pure market competition, but a mixed system of legally crafted and regulated non-state forms of property, production, exchange and consumption. According to Linz and Stepan, state-directed command economies are incompatible with democracy. Not only do they squeeze the life out of political societies. State-directed production and exchange also robs civil society of a vital support. A non-trivial degree of ownership diversity and market autonomy, in short, is necessary 'to produce the independence and liveliness of civil society so that it can make its contribution to a democracy'.[20]

*   *   *

Most contemporary discussions of civil society – the best recent collection of contributions is no exception[21] – seem uninterested in normative-philosophical questions. Civil society is viewed (among its friends) as a given good. The 'authority' or normative superiority of a state-protected civil society compared with other types of social and political regime is consequently presumed in quiet, or it is blindly taken for granted. Such presumption in effect leaves the contemporary protagonists of civil society with no plausible arguments, and it is one key reason why the current renaissance of the language of civil society remains intellectually and politically vulnerable, why it is bound to hearten cynics, and why the renaissance may well disappoint or even discredit its proponents.

My own work has tried to anticipate and reduce this normative vulnerability of the civil society perspective through two old, and one new, lines of argument. A plausible version of the two old arguments is well presented in G.W.F. Hegel's *Grundlinien der Philosophie des Rechts* (1821).[22] The first has to do with the temporality of civil society. In contrast to

---

[20] Juan J. Linz and Alfred Stepan, *Problems of Democratic Transition and Consolidation*, op. cit., pp. 7–9.
[21] John A. Hall (ed.), *Civil Society: Theory, History, Comparison* (Cambridge, UK and Cambridge, Mass., 1995). I am most grateful to John Hall for providing insightful remarks on an earlier draft of the following few pages.
[22] All citations are drawn from G.W.F. Hegel, *Grundlinien der Philosophie des Rechts* (Frankfurt am Main, 1976). Translations are my own.

those who conceive civil society as a 'natural' condition of human freedom, Hegel understood civil society (*bürgerliche Gesellschaft*) as a *historically produced* sphere of ethical life which comprises the economy, social classes, corporations and institutions concerned with the administration of welfare (*Polizei*) and civil law. The 'system of needs' stimulated by civil society in this sense decisively separates the human condition from the natural environment. Needs multiply and diversify, making it clear that civil society is not a pregiven and invariable substratum of life existing outside of space and time. Civil society is rather the outcome, the resultant of a long and complex process of historical transformation. 'The creation of civil society is the achievement of the modern world'. But civil society – this is Hegel's second compelling point – is also *wreckable*. In other words: there is no necessary identity or harmony among the various elements of civil society. Harmony nourished by unadulterated love may be achievable in households, but not in civil society, which is itself a mixed blessing. Its multiple forms of interaction and collective solidarity are often incommensurable, fragile and subject to serious – violent – conflict. Modern civil society is a restless battlefield where interest meets interest. It unfolds and develops in an arbitrary, blind, semi-spontaneous manner. This means not only that civil society cannot overcome its own particularities, but also that it tends to paralyse and undermine its own pluralism. As Hegel says, the exuberant development of one part of civil society may, and often does, impede or oppress its other parts, which is why civil society cannot remain or become 'civil' unless it is ordered politically.

*   *   *

This potentially self-destructive or wreckable quality of modern forms of civil society prompts a new line of argument. Inevitably, it raises the question of what after all is so good about civil society. Why cherish it as a practical accomplishment, or as an ideal? Are there any good and compelling reasons why it should be supported? These questions must be faced squarely and answered honestly, initially by recognizing that actually existing civil societies themselves force such questions upon their members. Civil societies constantly throw into doubt the conventional meanings and the accepted obviousness of social relationships. Civil societies promote an attitude of self-reflexivity, by which I mean the shared understanding among socially interacting and socially interconnected subjects that their world never stands still, that it is a puzzling product of their own making, and that as subjects of inquiry into the meaning of life they are an intrinsic part of the object of their enquiries. Civil societies permanently heap doubt on the standard objection, famously expressed by Georg Lukács among others, that modern capitalist societies constantly smash, replace and leave behind them the apparently irresistible bonds of the 'natural' world, only to create a kind of 'second nature' which evolves with exactly the same inexorable necessity of the irrational forces of the natural world.[23]

Civil societies certainly secrete ideologies that have this effect. They have done so from the beginning. The growth of modern civil societies, Trentmann has pointed out, is due in no small measure to the energies of groups, such as missionary movements and religious and trade union associations, that fought for their right to survive and thrive as *civil* associations by using universalist language that threatened the principle of plurality upon which civil societies thrive.[24] *Democracy and Civil Society* and *Civil Society and the State* pointed to numerous examples of specifically modern ideologies – such as patriarchal domination, the fetish of market competition and the ideology of socialism – that have taken root in civil society. The ideologies of nationalism and the conventional belief in 'the public' are new examples to be considered later in this book. So it is true that from time to time civil societies generate self-paralysing ideologies. But all hitherto existing and present-day civil societies contain powerful countertrends that ensure that 'society' has no fixed and immutable meaning. Víctor Pérez-Díaz has helpfully observed that the infinity and

[23] Georg Lukács, 'Reification and the Consciousness of the Proletariat', in *History and Class Consciousness* (Cambridge, Mass., 1971), pp. 83–122.
[24] In email correspondence from Princeton, New Jersey, dated 20 January 1998. I am most grateful to Frank Trentmann for many other thought-provoking comments on an earlier draft of parts of this book.

inquietude of the sea is a fitting symbol of modern civil societies, but the naturalistic image he chooses is not quite right.[25]
Civil societies destroy faith in the supposedly *natural* artifice
of 'Society'. They even stimulate awareness (evident in various forms of ecological thinking) that humanity itself may be
a threat to the self-sufficient freedom of the natural world
upon which civil society itself depends. Civil societies encourage their members to be suspicious of attempts to 'mytholo-
gize' (as Barthes would have said) their own social condition.
Civil societies enable their members to see through civil society – to label it *this* society, *our* society.

* * *

If that is so, then it becomes imperative to bring theorizations
of civil society in line with the self-reflexivity of actually existing civil societies. Their denaturalizing tendencies must be
made to boomerang back upon the language of civil society
itself. In other words, it becomes mandatory to recognize that
Hegel's comments on the embattled quality of the world of
civil society apply also to the concept of civil society. The history of modern theorizations of civil society is the history of
the quiet destruction of the philosophically naïve view that
the category of civil society perfectly represents some determinate reality existing 'out there'. The 'language' of civil society – 'language' is used throughout this book as a convenient
metaphor – increasingly speaks in tongues, in accordance with
different rules of grammar and conflicting vocabularies. Indeed, since the last quarter of the eighteenth century there
has been a burgeoning history of disputation about the philo-
sophical-normative status of the term. Some thinkers (Georg
Forster, Thomas Paine) have considered civil society to be the
earthly expression of God-given natural rights. Others interpret the concept within the framework of a theory of history
that supposes either that civil society is a moment in the actualization of the ethical idea, of mind (*Geist*) actively working its way into the existing world (Hegel); or (as Marx and

[25] Víctor Pérez-Díaz, *The Return of Civil Society: The Emergence of Democratic Spain* (Cambridge, Mass., and London, 1993), p. 62.

others within the communist tradition supposed) that civil society is a moment in the development and overcoming of modern, class-ridden bourgeois society. There are some (an example is Emile Durkheim's *'L'Allemagne au-dessus de tout'. La mentalité germanique et la guerre* [1915]) who instead consider civil society as a spontaneous group-centred expression of 'loving-kindness and fraternity', values that have an elective affinity with the patterns of organic solidarity of industrial society. And there are thinkers (steeped in the originally conservative reverence for tradition) who interpret civil society as a customary, time-bound ensemble of institutions that certainly count as an invention of the modern world, but an invention that is confined to certain regions of the earth and does not enjoy any metahistorical guarantee that it will flourish, or even survive.

These are just samples of the bewildering plurality of normative justifications of civil society, but their listing is enough to understand why some critics have been tempted into the conclusion that exercises in justification are bound to fail because the concept of civil society is a muddled, 'essentially contested' term that amounts to nothing but two misguided nonsense words. This type of argument plausibly highlights the polysemic quality of the civil society perspective. But it tends in practice to flirt with the politically dangerous predilection to give up on civil society, to admit 'civil society fatigue', to succumb to the temptation to look elsewhere for public or private salvation. Not only that, but those who emphasize the 'muddled' or 'babbling' quality of the language of civil society prematurely abandon the possibility of normatively justifying civil society in fresh, exciting ways. In particular, they fail to see that the plural structures of a civil society can be – and are best – expressed through a type of *post-foundationalist* normative justification that itself recognizes, and actively reinforces respect for, the multiplicity of often incommensurable normative codes and forms of contemporary social life. The term 'civil society' is a signifier of plurality. It therefore must attempt to break with the bad monist habit of philosophically justifying civil society by referring back to a substantive grounding principle, such as the early modern notions of God-given justice, natural rights or the principle of utility, or their later modern counterparts of rational argumentation (Habermas), principles of 'the right to equal concern and respect' (Dworkin), respect for 'the worth of the individual' (Hall), or knowledge of a 'good which we can know in common' (Sandel).

During the past two decades, my reflections on civil society and related topics have aimed to raise a new question: Can a democratic theory of civil society live without such found-ationalist assumptions? Can civil society come to be seen by those who enjoy or envy it as a system of structured social interaction guided by a 'higher amorality' (Niklas Luhmann) that discourages moralizing, bigotry and power grabbing, and encourages a politics that refuses to judge its opponents as 'enemies'? Can the concept of civil society itself symbolically express the point that, in the absence of plausible Universals, it too must learn the art of living in a world marked by flux and ambiguity?

The gist of my tentative responses to these questions is that the theory of civil society cannot be treated as a universal language game in the traditional sense. It is incapable of know-ing everything, refuting its opponents with talk of Absolutes, and urging on the world universal commitment to a Grand Ideal which makes possible the practical synthesis of all dif-ferences: for instance, through a shared definition of the quin-tessential nature and merits of Civil Society. In my early critique of Habermas's theory of communication, as well as in the immanent critique of Jean-François Lyotard's *La Condition post-moderne*,[26] the theory of civil society is understood as an im-plied condition and practical consequence of philosophical and political pluralism, which is not itself an ethical First Prin-ciple, but is better understood in terms of the logic of occa-sion, as it was first practised among the pre-Socratics. This is to say that the theory of civil society understands itself as merely one normatively inclined theory among others. It hum-bly sees itself as one possible approach that nevertheless boldly

---

[26] John Keane, *Public Life and Late Capitalism* (Cambridge and New York, 1984); and 'The Modern Democratic Revolution: Reflections on Lyotard's *The Postmodern Condition*', in Andrew Benjamin (ed.), *Judging Lyotard* (London and New York, 1992), pp. 81–98.

accentuates the need for giving greater emphasis to both theoretical pluralism and a political project bent on enabling a genuinely non-hierarchical plurality of individuals and groups openly and non-violently to express their solidarity with – and opposition to – each other's ideals and ways of life.

This post-foundationalist understanding of civil society takes care of the relativist objection that civil society is perforce a pseudo-universal category of the liberal-individualist West.[27] Relativists suppose that forms of life (as Wittgenstein would say) are divided by unbridgeable differences, and that this is so because they are unavoidably determined by different forces of which they are often unaware, and which they have little power to reshape. The form of life called civil society belongs to the liberal-individualist West: the rest of the world cannot know or experience anything of it. So relativism is prone to moralism. It is driven to say that if 'the West' enjoys civil society and the Other suffers barbarism, for instance, then so be it. Civil society is for Us. Anything else is for Them.

This relativist objection is full of confusions. Quite aside from tumbling into a self-contradiction – it *knows* that terms like civil society are always specific to particular contexts – the relativist displays an imperialist attitude towards 'the West', as if those who lived there agreed unanimously on the meaning of the term 'civil society', which they most certainly do not. Relativists also ignore the various ways in which various (originally European) definitions of civil society are presently spreading to all four corners of the earth, which is to say in this case that relativists have not understood that the world is in the process of rejecting relativism. The Chinese case cited above suggests as well that relativists overlook the possibility that the self-reflexive, self-organizing non-governmental organizations that some call civil society can and do live by other names in other linguistic and cultural milieux. And relativism – here its evident weakness is fatal – usually implies that the 'foreign' context it wants to protect against the bad 'Western' category of

<hr />

[27] See the interesting (if ramshackle) remarks on the problem of relativism and universalism in Chris Hann, 'Introduction: Political Society and Civil Anthropology', in Chris Hann and Elizabeth Dunn (eds) *Civil Society: Challenging Western Models* (London and New York, 1996), pp. 17–24.

civil society has *essentially Other* principles of organization. That presumption mistakenly supposes that the Other has never borrowed anything from anywhere else in the past, and that today it is an undivided, essentially harmonious and stable entity. This is bad news indeed for those individuals, groups and organizations within that context who do not enjoy the fruits of non-violent toleration of differences, and which they could only ever enjoy if they were secured through the *universal* requirement of a functioning civil society that is guaranteed, protected and enhanced by political-legal institutions.

The post-foundationalist understanding of civil society also takes care of the objection that the old ideal of civil society nowadays resembles a drunk wandering in darkness in search of a lamppost; or, as Adam Seligman has more soberly put it, that the early modern notions of civil society, which rested upon beliefs 'in Godly benevolence and in natural sympathy . . . are no longer ours to share, and we can no longer use them to construct our models of the social order'.[28] The post-foundationalist understanding of civil society also overcomes the objection that the very term 'civil society' is polluted by its diverse and contradictory meanings. Paradoxically, the post-foundationalist understanding of civil society that I am trying to develop insists that the meaning and ethical significance of civil society at any given time and place can be asserted and/ or contested as such only within a sociopolitical framework marked by the separation of civil and state institutions, whose power to shape the lives of citizens is subject permanently to mechanisms that enable disputation, accountability and representation. In other words, the normatively inclined procedures of civil society – for instance, the legally guaranteed freedom of civil association and a plurality of communications media not controlled by state actors – are a *conditio sine qua non* of a life without ethico-philosophical or political Foundations. Whoever rejects civil society as an ideal and as a practical achievement knowingly or unknowingly falls back into the trap of foundationalism and its moralizing faith in Truth and Ethics. Or else they plummet into a cynical and

[28] Adam B. Seligman, *The Idea of Civil Society* (New York and Toronto, 1992), pp. 205–6.

self-contradictory relativism, which insists that there are no certain or preferable guidelines in life, thereupon displaying the same logical and political muddle as the Cretan Epimenides, who truthfully declared that all Cretans were liars.

* * *

There are certain trends within contemporary philosophy that assist the birth of this new, post-foundationalist justification of civil society. Consider the example of Richard Rorty's pragmatism, which is driven by the thought that modern democratic revolutions will be remembered, if they are remembered at all, for their highlighting of the fact that social and political institutions *can* be viewed as experiments in cooperation, rather than as attempts to embody a timeless universal order. Rorty rejects the 'Enlightenment idea of "reason"', according to which moral truth corresponds to the ahistorical essence of humanity, thereby ensuring that free and open discussion produces 'one right answer' to moral as well as to scientific questions. Rorty cites Jefferson's preamble to the Virginia Statute for Religious Freedom as an example of this specious Enlightenment postulate: 'truth is great and will prevail if left to herself, . . . she is the proper and sufficient antagonist to error, and has nothing to fear from the conflict, unless by human interposition disarmed of her natural weapons, free argument and debate, errors ceasing to be dangerous when it is permitted freely to contradict them.'[29]

Rorty points out that Jefferson was not altogether consistent in his rationalist defence of truth. There is another – pragmatically inclined – Jefferson who suspended his belief in truth and called for a truce among conflicting, previously warring definitions of truth. This Jeffersonian compromise, evident in his famous remark that 'it does me no injury for my neighbor to say that there are twenty Gods or no God', opened up the possibility that politics can be separated from beliefs about matters that are alleged to be of ultimate importance. It implied that shared beliefs among citizens on such matters are not essential to an open society, that what would later be called

[29] Thomas Jefferson, *Notes on the State of Virginia*, Query XVII, in A.A. Lipscomb and A.E. Bergh (eds), *The Writings of Thomas Jefferson* (Washington, DC, 1905), vol. 2, p. 302.

republican democracy rested upon a higher 'amorality': an agreement to disagree about matters of conscience.

Rorty favours this kind of Jeffersonian pragmatism for two tightly related reasons. To begin with, Rorty insists that the theory of truth championed by the early modern Enlightenment has been discredited. The rationalist presumption that religion, myth, tradition and other prejudices could be swept away by knowledge of something timelessly and quintessentially human has finally been exposed as unwarranted arrogance. 'Anthropologists and historians of science have blurred the distinction between innate rationality and the products of acculturation', writes Rorty.

> Philosophers such as Heidegger and Gadamer have given us ways of seeing human beings as historical all the way through. Other philosophers, such as Quine and Davidson, have blurred the distinction between permanent truths of reason and temporary truth of fact. Psychoanalysis has blurred the distinction between conscience and the emotions of love, hate, and fear, and thus the distinction between morality and prudence.

Rorty concludes: 'The result is to erase the picture of the self common to Greek metaphysics, Christian theology, and Enlightenment rationalism: the picture of an ahistorical natural center, the locus of human dignity, surrounded by an adventitious and inessential periphery.'[30]

Rorty proceeds from this observation to a second reason for favouring the Jeffersonian compromise. Only by means of such a compromise, he argues, can the devils of dogmatism be cast out from the body politic. To bolster this claim, Rorty relies upon what might be called his moral indifference principle, which states that due to the discrediting of the many different and competing quests for Truth, the subject of truth has become uninteresting and should therefore be set aside as irrelevant in social and political matters. Even philosophy should

[30] Richard Rorty, 'The Priority of Democracy to Philosophy', in Richard Rorty, *Objectivity, Relativism, and Truth: Philosophical Papers* (Cambridge, 1991), vol. 1, p. 176. See also his 'Philosophy as Science, as Metaphor, and as Politics', in *Essays on Heidegger and Others* (Cambridge and New York, 1991).

lose its crown as reigning monarch of the human (and bio-natural) sciences. Philosophy is no longer entitled to make the arrogant claim to be a know-all, to be the commander of the search for truth about a prior and independent order. Philosophy should step down and step aside – just as other forms of life ought to so do – by acknowledging that the human condition is happiest when it is tolerant of differences of opinion, speech and ways of life. That in turn requires working for what Rorty calls a 'post-Philosophical culture'. Such a society is prefigured in the decline and abandonment of philosophy. Men and women feel themselves to be on their own, merely finite beings, with no links to something Beyond. They sense that all criteria are no more than 'temporary resting places';[31] and they understand that there is nothing deep down inside us save for what we have put there ourselves, no criterion that we have not created in the course of creating a practice, no standard of rationality that is not an appeal to such a criterion, no rigorous argumentation that is not obedience to our own conventions. These 'postmodern' men and women grasp that controversies about the world are won or lost or brought to a halt through a process of jousting among storytelling interlocutors. These jousts use all the tricks in the book of persuasion and deception. They try to make their opponents look uninformed, implausible, foolish or worse by deploying rhetoric, by means of recontextualization, strong misreadings and other communicative strategies.

* * *

The democratic perspectives on civil society and state institutions that I have been developing obviously share certain theoretical and political affinities with Rorty's rejection of philosophy. The two projects are bonded by suspicion of ideologies, opposition to the cruel hubris they bring into the world, and a positive vision of democratic pluralism. Both are certainly repelled by the Orwellian image of 'a boot stamping down on a human face, forever'. But – viewed from the civil society perspective – Rorty's work nevertheless harbours

[31] Richard Rorty, *Consequences of Pragmatism (Essays: 1972–1980)* (Minneapolis, 1982), p. xlii.

difficulties that directly feed its *pre-political* quality. Rorty tells us that democratic institutions cannot be combined with the sense of common purpose predemocratic societies enjoyed. He warns us that it is hard to be both enamoured of one version of the world – to be an ideologist – and to be tolerant of all others. Following Dewey, he presumes that there are no goods achieved by earlier civilizations and regimes that would be worth retrieving if the price to be paid was a reduction of democracies' propensity to 'leave people alone, to let them try out their private visions of perfection in peace'.[32] And he draws from this the apparently self-consistent conclusion that not even democracy can be considered a universal, even though it is the *conditio sine qua non* of pluralism. As an ideal, democracy has neither theological nor ontological foundations. There are no First Principles of democracy. It can get along nicely without philosophical presuppositions. All that can be said about democracy, where it exists, is that it is a system that accords with 'the moral intuitions of the particular historical community that has created those institutions'.

* * *

The trouble with this line of reasoning, which owes more to Hume than it does to Kant, is that it risks falling into a relativist abyss. Rorty's argument that questions of truth about foundations should be dropped and that democracy – a system that underwrites the ability of neighbours to say that there is no God, or that there are twenty gods – is only good because it is viewed as a *contextually specific* good (Rawls) is unsatisfactory. The claim that democracy is good only when the historically constituted 'moral intuitions' (or what he calls elsewhere the 'settled social habits') of a political community consider it as good reduces democracy to the status of merely one ideal among others. And that means that if, within a community, toleration and pity are in short supply, or even that other 'moral intuitions' – a term that is both left undefined and reminiscent of Hume's concept of 'opinion' – are unfriendly towards democracy, then that is unfortunate for demo-

[32] Ibid., p. 194.

crats elsewhere. Democrats who are not members of that non-
democratic community are not entitled to stick their noses
into others' business. If they try to do so, they are in effect
acting as if they were Keepers and Propagators of the Truth.
They would commit a contradiction. Better then to understand democracy as a historically specific invention without
any special regional or global status – and certainly without
any right to intervene in anti-democratic contexts. Despite
Rorty's own uncharacteristic assertion (in the 1993 Oxford
Amnesty lecture) that 'the culture of human rights' is 'mor-
ally superior to other cultures',[33] democracy has to live with
those who are unfriendly towards democracy. It has to tolerate the intolerant. It has to take pity on those who know no
pity.

Rorty's argument slides at this point into a contradictory
muddle, which is compounded by a second, and related, difficulty that stems from his political wistfulness. Rorty tells us
little or nothing about the organizing principles – the proce-
dural rules – of democratic institutions, as if to attempt to do
so risks a relapse into foundationalist temptations. The dangers of such a relapse are well taken. But there is another kind
of danger – that of political wistfulness and, thus, blasé silence
about the *institutional preconditions* of democracy – that goes
unrecognized in Rorty's otherwise compelling commentaries.
The best that he can do is to appeal to the importance of
pragmatism: to work towards the 'end of ideology' by encouraging citizens and politicians to be aware that they are heirs to
the same historical traditions, that they need to practise give-
and-take between shared intuitions about the consequences
of adopting particular actions and intuitions about general
principles, with neither having the determining voice.

Rorty is not alone in this. Political wistfulness seems to have
reached almost epidemic proportions in contemporary post-
foundationalist thinking. Elsewhere I have criticized Lyotard's
pre-political assertion of the need for 'marvelling at the diver-

[33] Richard Rorty, 'Human Rights, Rationality, and Sentimentality', in Susan
Hurley and Steven Shute (eds), *Human Rights* (New York, 1993), pp. 112–
34.

sity of discursive species, just as we do at the diversity of plant and animal species'. And I have favourably compared certain Czech strands of anti-totalitarian political thinking during the Brezhnev period with the later Heidegger's polemics against the modern world, including his retreatist call 'to prepare to be prepared for the manifestation of God, or for the absence of God as things go downhill all the way'.[34] To this list could be added earlier twentieth-century examples, like the mature Wittgenstein's asinine empathy for Stalinism and his simultaneous insistence that philosophy should leave everything as it is. Another example is Ernst Jünger's cold-blooded detachment from the turmoil around him, his tergiversation after experiencing first-hand the murderous nihilism of the Third Reich, and his later embrace of the anti-political principle of *désinvolture*, the cheerful, free-and-easy nonchalance of the intellectual aristocrat. The same kind of political wistfulness continues to surface in contemporary political philosophy. Alasdair MacIntyre's conclusion (in *After Virtue*) that we are now 'waiting not for a Godot, but for another – doubtless very different – St Benedict'[35] is an example; and so too is Michel Foucault's identification of philosophy with 'precisely the challenging of all phenomena of domination' and his affirmation of the nebulously defined project of giving 'one's self . . . the techniques of management' that would allow 'games of power to be played with a minimum of domination'.[36]

There are no doubt different reasons (to do with context, thought patterns, styles of argumentation, and biography) why each of these thinkers goes off the political rails – or, to change metaphors, goes quiet on politics. The sources of Rorty's political wistfulness are not entirely clear. It is well known that

---

[34] See my 'The Modern Democratic Revolution: Reflections on Lyotard's *The Postmodern Condition*', op. cit.; and my forthcoming study of the life and times, and the aesthetic and political works of Václav Havel, tentatively entitled *The Temptations of Power* (London, Munich and New York, 1999).
[35] Alasdair MacIntyre, *After Virtue* (Notre Dame, 1981), p. 245.
[36] Michel Foucault, 'The Ethic of Care for the Self as a Practice of Freedom', in J. Bernauer and D. Rasmussen (eds), *The Final Foucault* (Boston, Mass., 1988), pp. 20, 18.

in the American context his political sympathies unfashionably lie with the New Deal project. There is also some textual evidence that it is traceable in part to his unreconstructed admiration for what he calls 'the American habit of giving democracy priority over philosophy' – traceable, that is to say, to his nation-bound feeling that Americans have discovered and put into practice what others (if they are lucky) are still thinking about and practically groping towards. This confidence appears to underpin his commitment to the moral indifference principle outlined above, which at best calls upon us to tolerate others' private predilections and to *withdraw* from ideological discussions and forms of life. 'We have to insist', writes Rorty, 'that not every argument needs to be met in the terms in which it is presented. Accommodation and tolerance must stop short of a willingness to work within any vocabulary that one's interlocutor wishes to use, to take seriously any topic that he puts forward for discussion.'

Rorty emphasizes that this requirement may lead us simply to *drop* questions and the vocabulary in which those questions are posed. His recommendation that we should do so is entirely consistent with dropping the belief in the possibility of a universal moral Esperanto. To which in reply it needs to be asked: Doesn't the moral indifference principle, with its call for toleration of differences, pity for those who suffer cruelty, and tactical withdrawals from the territory of ideology, presuppose, imply and require a certain ensemble of institutional arrangements, without which freedom from ideology is not possible? Don't such arrangements require – from all those who are happy to put up with such freedom, or who actively support it – a moral and political commitment to their preservation as such? And isn't such commitment to these arrangements potentially the object of theoretical reflection?

* * *

Certain types of answer to these questions flow readily from the tongues of those who stand within the civil society perspective. Anyone who talks of the need for tolerance of differences and freedom from ideology is already committed, whether they recognize it or not, to the construction, preservation and development of a pluralistic and state-protected civil society, whose rich heterarchy and thriving agonistic pluralism, mediated by parapolitical bodies, such as political parties and parliaments, together ensure that hubris is checkable. The converse equally applies: anyone who does not recognize the need for these institutions of civil society, state and their intermediaries, or who works actively against them, even to destroy them, is no friend of pluralism – and perhaps even its dangerous enemy. The institutional arrangement of an open, pluralistic civil society protected and nurtured by publicly accountable state mechanisms is (to speak in Kantian terms) a transcendental-logical condition of democracy. This precondition can, of course, be actively resisted or violently destroyed by human actors, in which case democratic pluralism is unsafe, or exterminated. But otherwise this precondition must be considered a *universal* rule that *must* be followed if the differences among a variety of individuals, groups, institutions, even whole civilizations, are to be tolerated peacefully. The principle of toleration cannot be applied to itself. Civil society, to put it simply, is either an actual or anticipated *a priori* of the struggle for egalitarian diversity, and those who practically deny this *a priori* are monists – and most likely bigots, bullies, tyrants or totalitarians.

Disputes

In the various new applications of the language of civil society sketched above can be seen signs of the end of a long century of political thinking dominated by statist ideologies like Bolshevism, fascism, social democracy and Third World liberation. The theme of civil society has been reborn on a grand scale, and it can be said without much exaggeration that it has moved to occupy the centre-ground of contemporary political thought. This development was wholly unexpected and it has consequently filled some with the millenarian hope that the Age of Civil Society is nigh.[1] That expectation should be resisted, for it is important to stress once again the sober caveat defended in the first two volumes on civil society: those who call for a new civil society paradigm, or who think of it politically as a substitute for unconvincing or dying ideologies like socialism, nationalism and Third World liberation, risk turning civil society into an ideological concept. The attempt to form a grand theoretical explanation of the past, present and future relationships between civil societies and states, and to combine within that explanation the three different usages of the term 'civil society' outlined above, is not merely inappropriate, but wholly undesirable. If attempted, it would entrap usages of the language of civil society within a per-

[1] See, for example, the early argument for a 'neo-Copernican revolution' in favour of civil society against the state in Jean-Marie Benoist, *Les Outils de la liberté* (Paris, 1985).

formative contradiction – a language sensitive to complexity and openness would become simple and close-minded – and it would thereby paralyse its radically pluralist and democratic potential.

A theoretical 'metadiscourse' or 'grand narrative' on civil society would almost certainly hypostatize the civil society–state distinction, endowing it perhaps with falsely anthropomorphic qualities. It would probably result in glib philosophical generalizations, oversimplified sociological observations and misguided or dogmatic political recommendations and tactics. So the intellectual point of clarifying the currently confused and overlapping usages of the concept of civil society should be altogether more modest: every effort should be made to fashion the current renaissance of civil society into an *interpretative standpoint* which can be of some utility in historical inquiries, sociological investigations, normative discussions and the making of political judgments. This more modest understanding of the category of civil society acknowledges its deeply contestable character. This fate it necessarily shares with every other key concept in the human sciences, which is to say that permanent attention must be given to what the term can and cannot achieve, to the areas of inquiry in which it might fruitfully be applied, as well as to its past and present weaknesses and probable future limits.

*   *   *

Among the duties of the friends of civil society is to understand better why it has its detractors and outright enemies, and to foster greater clarity about the concept's potential weak points, silences and outright vulnerability. The contemporary movement of the language of civil society towards the heart of the human sciences, like all intellectual shifts, is certainly encountering active resistance. Controversies have been heated and opposition has been stiff, so spirited in fact that at times it seems to have had the paradoxical effect of turning ever more heads in the direction of the subject of civil society. The enemies and critics of civil society seem unwittingly to confirm its present-day intellectual and political centrality. They are cast in the strange role of fellow travellers and advocates of a spreading phenomenon which they themselves doubt, openly suspect or actively detest.

It is true that the criticisms of the state–civil society distinction are of uneven quality. At least some of those who have refused to speak the language of civil society seem to base their objections on half-readings, wilful misreadings or no reading of the literature on the subject. The objection that civil society is seen by its anarchistic friends as free of freedom-killing institutional restraints, that a civil society comprises 'shapeless congeries of decisions between mutually consenting private persons', and that therefore 'the myth of civil society is a tale of a noncoercive political order', is of this type.[2] So too is the objection, typically launched by state-minded social democratic thinkers and friends and fellow-travellers and nostalgics of the former Soviet-type regimes, that the civil society project is in effect hostile to all forms of state institutions.[3] It is tempting to take that type of criticism *cum grano salis*, since – the points have been sketched above – it ignores the late-twentieth-century decline of all forms of *étatisme* and is so obviously trapped in an impoverished zero-sum understanding of the state–civil society relationship. One point only is worth repeating to these critics: there *are* contexts, such as the emergence of Solidarność in Poland in 1980, where the 'stateness' of a state is reduced the more civil society gains ground. But that is certainly far from the norm. Far more common are contexts in which weak

[2] G. M. Tamás, 'A Disquisition on Civil Society', *Social Research*, vol. 61, no. 2 (Summer 1994), p. 216. Similar criticisms of the 'anarcho-Foucauldian' aims of my perspectives on civil society and state institutions are made by Nicholas Garnham in 'Comments on John Keane's "Structural Transformations of the Public Sphere"', *The Communication Review*, vol. 1, no. 1 (1995), pp. 23–5. See also Keith Tester's strangely deconstructionist use of Marx to attack the 'myth' of civil society, which he understands as 'the milieu of private contractual relationships', in *Civil Society* (London and New York, 1992).

[3] Krishan Kumar, 'Civil Society: An Inquiry into the Usefulness of an Historical Term', *British Journal of Sociology*, vol. 44 (1993), pp. 375–96. See the reply by C.G.A. Bryant, 'Social Self-Organization, Civility and Sociology: A Comment on Kumar's "Civil Society"', *British Journal of Sociology*, vol. 44 (1993), pp. 397–401; and the debate that ensued in the same journal, vol. 45 (1994).

states and weak civil societies produce implosion and collapse, leading to uncivil war; the failed states of contemporary Afghanistan, Yugoslavia and Algeria are examples. More common as well are those contexts, such as the old democracies of the north Atlantic region, in which states can and do govern effectively exactly because they enable their strong civil societies to reproduce and thrive, at times in opposition to cramping state bureaucracies.

Easily the loudest criticism so far of the language of civil society has come from within the shrinking circles of Marxism. *Democracy and Civil Society* and *Civil Society and the State* were targeted in part at Marxism-Leninism. They took special aim at the regimes of 'actually existing socialism', and more generally at any and every form of actually existing Leftism or Leftist thinking that paid little or no attention to the state–civil society distinction. Some reviewers and readers correctly spotted that the volumes tenaciously remained 'on the Left' – and even a few ungenerous critics condescendingly described them as examples of 'left-wing Thatcherism'. Less often appreciated was the key point that the descriptions of these works as 'on the Left' applied only because I was attempting to effect something of a Copernican revolution in the meaning of the Left–Right distinction. To be an intellectual or political sympathizer or activist of the Left, I argued, is to recognize the complexity of the world, to suspect and reject ideologies of every kind, to see the need to democratize the idea of socialism through the prism of the old state–civil society distinction, and to be in favour of social and political systems that display a rich plurality of self-governing civil society institutions legally administered by, and held accountable to, democratically organized state institutions.[4]

*   *   *

It comes as little surprise that some comrades on the Left objected to my project. The most swingeing attack came from

---

[4] John Keane, 'Democracy and the Decline of the Left', the introduction to Norberto Bobbio, *Democracy and Dictatorship: The Nature and Limits of State Power* (Cambridge, 1989), pp. vii–xxviii.

Ellen Meiksins Wood. The contours of her position were first sketched at a conference (at which we both spoke) organized by the Yugoslav League of Communists in Cavtat, near Dubrovnik, in October 1988, just months before that country was ripped apart by nationalist ideology and force of arms.[5] It is worth noting that Wood's position was counter-revolutionary. Some Yugoslav comrades were ecstatic. At precisely the moment when totalitarian socialism was beginning to collapse, she tried to demonstrate that the advocates of 'civil society' were recoiling from the ugly realities of the present, in effect by attempting 'to conceptualize away the problem of capitalism'. According to Wood, civil society, 'an all-purpose catchword for the left', is a term that has come to be a positive synonym for voluntary association, diversity and liberty, when it is in fact better used to describe and to judge 'the totalizing logic and the coercive power of capitalism'. Wood implicitly acknowledged the normative point that all socialists, Marxist or otherwise, should uphold 'the principles of legality, freedom of speech and association, and the protection of a "non-state" sphere against incursions by the state'. But – Wood argued – these principles are already specified by, and incorporated within, the Marxist approach, whose genuine strength consists in its hard-nosed insistence that the very division between civil society and the state is expressive of capitalism.

Wood proved to be an author's dream. Against my original charge that the Marxist account of modern civil societies is guided by monistic, reductionist and economistic thinking, she insisted on the very point which is the most vulnerable: that property-driven relations of exploitation and domination 'irreducibly *constitute* civil society, not just as some alien and

[5] Ellen Meiksins Wood, ' "Civil Society" and the Devaluation of Democracy', a paper delivered at the Roundtable '88, 'Socialism and the "Spiritual Situation of the Age" ', Cavtat, Yugoslavia, 20–3 October 1988. A revised and expanded version appeared as 'The Uses and Abuses of "Civil Society" ', *The Socialist Register 1990* (London, 1990), pp. 60–84. A crude version of Wood's argument is evident in the attack on my 'poetic', middle-class defence of 'nice people' and 'nice associations' in Colin Sparks, *Communism, Capitalism and the Mass Media* (London, 1998), chapter 5.

correctible disorder but as its very essence, the particular structure of domination and coercion that is specific to capitalism
as a systemic totality'. The key analytic-empirical point is that
civil society is a particular social form unique to the modern
world. Civil society, Wood concluded,

> has given private property and its possessors a command over
> people and their daily lives, a power accountable to no one,
> which many an old tyrannical state would have envied. Those
> activities and experiences which fall outside the immediate
> command structure of the capitalist enterprise, or outside the
> political power of capital, are regulated by the dictates of the
> market, the necessities of competition and profitability.

Wood then added a caveat:

> Even when the market is not, as it commonly is in advanced
> capitalist societies, merely an instrument of power for giant
> conglomerates and multinational corporations, it is still a coer-
> cive force, capable of subjecting all human values, activities
> and relationships to its imperatives. No ancient despot could
> have hoped to penetrate the personal lives of its subjects –
> their choices, preferences, and relationships – in the same com-
> prehensive and minute detail, not only in the workplace but in
> every corner of their lives.

Her conclusion was as straightforward as it was blunt: 'It is
perhaps time for us in the West to tell a few home truths
about capitalism, instead of hiding them discreetly behind the
screen of "civil society".'

*   *   *

A more sophisticated neo-Marxist line of criticism is that of
Mark Neocleous, who attempts to provide an immanent critique of my version of the 'civil society' approach. Neocleous
fears (without foundation, I think) that my approach de-
values the empirical-analytic importance of the category of
the state, but he goes on to argue (correctly) that the concept
of the state is meaningful only if and when it is used in con-
junction with 'civil society', and vice versa. The state–civil

society distinction is then used to criticize certain strands of Marxism which have either ignored the distinction or confined it (like Ellen Meiksins Wood) within a crudely economistic base-superstructure model. Following Poulantzas, Neocleous proposes that states have a 'constitutive power' over civil society. The state is not simply an epiphenomenon of class relations and class conflict. The case study of English politics after 1832 provided by Neocleous suggests that political administration has the threefold effect of constituting legal subjectivity, fashioning the market, and subsuming class conflict into the structures of the state. It follows from this typology of political administration that there can be no adequate theory of the state that is not simultaneously an analysis of its presence in 'the constitution and reproduction of the relations of production'. From his point of view, the state is interpreted as an apparatus that is both formed through class struggles within civil society and *administers* those struggles by means of 'political administration'.[6]

Neocleous makes clear that modern civil society (*bürgerliche Gesellschaft*) comprises more than commodity production and exchange, that it is both civil (the term is poorly defined by him) and 'essentially bourgeois' – it is a sphere driven by the ideal of atomized self-seeking individuals and the reality of conflicts between wage labour and capital. It is this 'essentially bourgeois' quality of modern civil society that explains why it is historically specific, and why its future abolition is both thinkable and politically desirable. According to Neocleous, 'the communist project should be conceived not as the "revitalization" of civil society, but its overcoming, along with the state, a project of the socialization of the political and politicization of the social for which Marx's concept of the *social*, theoretically distinct from his concept of civil society, has an explicitly critical edge'.[7]

* * *

[6] Mark Neocleous, *Administering Civil Society: Towards a Theory of State Power* (New York, 1996), pp. vii–viii; and the introduction to Nicos Poulantzas, *State, Power, Socialism* (London, 1980).
[7] *Administering Civil Society*, op. cit., p. x.

What are the friends of civil society to make of all this theorizing? There is no doubt that these neo-Marxian interpretations of the modern state–civil society relationship contain some fruitful insights. They remind us that political freedom, as Marx argued against Bruno Bauer and others, is not the same as social freedom. The Marxian-inspired account also correctly emphasized – against Paine, Forster and others – that the living group networks of modern civil societies are not somehow 'natural', as if they could escape the demands of time and function only according to spontaneous adaptations. By emphasizing the historically specific character of the civil society–state relationship, Marx and his followers correctly pointed to the undemocratic forms of class power harboured by modern civil societies. Wood also lashes out especially against those usages of the term 'civil society' that suppose that only state institutions are *coercive*. All these neo-Marxian points are useful. But I am convinced that the economism of the neo-Marxian approach, its presumption of a 'universal class', and its explicit commitment (echoed by Neocleous) to the Myth of Collective Harmony must all be rejected. Let us look at these three deficiencies in more detail.

Those attracted by some version of the Marxian interpretation explain the power relations of civil societies mainly in terms of forces and relations of *production*. Modern times are analysed in terms of the simplifying *idealtypisch* dichotomy of economic or political (and ideological) structures. The institutional complexity of civil society is thereby concealed. The crucially important dynamics, past and present, of *other* forms of civil life, such as households, communications media, voluntary associations, professions and 'policing' institutions like hospitals, schools and prisons, are devalued. Marx's 'economistic' account of civil society also led him and subsequent Marxists to ignore the democratic potential of the type of citizens' associations cherished by Paine and Tocqueville. The Marxian lack of respect or enthusiasm for mechanisms such as the independent press, freedom of assembly and rights to vote – which were interpreted by Marx as the 'form' through which only bourgeois power is consolidated, rather than as a necessary condition of a post-bourgeois democracy – rendered

the Marxian idea of socialism vulnerable to political dictatorship. It encouraged its deliverance into the hands of revolu-
tionaries contemptuous of 'bourgeois freedom'. Encouraged
by Marx's view that 'none of the so-called rights of man [equal-
ity, liberty, security, property] goes beyond the egoistic man,
the man withdrawn into himself, his private interest and his
private choices and separated from the community as a member of civil society',[8] socialism became obsessed in practice
with snuffing out the *civil* roots of political democracy in the
name of eliminating 'capitalism'.

Another set of problems derives from Neocleous's reliance
upon Marx's anticipation of the abolition of the state and the
withering away of conflict in future communist society. Marx
believed that 'freedom consists in converting the state from
an organ superimposed upon society into one completely subordinate to it'.[9] He assumed that the successful struggle of the
working class for control over civil society would permit the
abolition of the state – and release a flood of free, creative
activity. Freedom for Marx did not consist in maximizing the
independence of self-governing subjects within a civil society
framed by political-legal institutions. It rather consisted in
smashing down the barriers between the social and political
spheres, thereby maximizing unity, harmony and self-fulfilment
among fully conscious and self-determining social individuals.
Marx (like Neocleous) supposed that state apparatuses could
and should be abolished and replaced by simple administrative organs. All communist beings would make decisions
on all public matters, no matter how insignificant, and without resorting to separate political-legal institutions for securing agreements or reconciling conflicts. Even the notion of
being a citizen – acting in concert with others to resist or
defend certain policy goals – would disappear.

Marx's attempted defence of a species of the nineteenth-
century Myth of Collective Harmony *presupposed* the central

[8] Karl Marx, 'On the Jewish Question', in *Writings of the Young Marx on
Philosophy and Society*, ed. Lloyd D. Easton and Kurt H. Guddat (Garden
City, 1967), pp. 236–7.
[9] 'Critique of the Gotha Programme', in *Selected Works*, vol. 3, p. 25.

role of the working class in the struggle for socialism. It failed to recognize that the democratic potential of workers within any particular context depends *not* upon the role as a historically privileged 'universal class' that they have been ascribed by some grand theory, but upon such factors as living historical traditions, modes of technology, the structure of industrial relations, patterns of state governance and the same workers' ability to form bonds of solidarity with other groups within civil society. Not only that: the Marxian urge to tip the state–civil society division into the dustbins of history never asked whether the social victories of workers against employers might well have led instead to the democratization of state institutions and the *preservation* and *democratic reform* of civil society. The possibility of a publicly accountable, state-guaranteed pluralist and democratically organized civil society – a civil society no longer dominated by commodity production and exchange – was unthinkable to Marx. Finally: Marx's vision of a future communist society in which no one would rule over anyone else, and in which power would amicably be exercised by all or, more accurately, by nobody, failed to see that political-legal institutions would always to some degree be necessary in a complex, democratic system. The inverse of this point is important: Marx failed to see that any and every complex society requires safeguards against the abuse of state and civil power so as to make it impossible for them to grow to alarming proportions. By anticipating a 'true democracy' in which 'the functions of government become simple administrative functions',[10] the Marxian theory (Neocleous and Wood included) consigned a whole tradition of theoretical reflection on the scope and limits of state power to the museums of 'bourgeois' prehistory.

* * *

Ernest Gellner's *Conditions of Liberty* provides a leathery response to contemporary Marxist attacks on civil society.[11]

---

[10] Karl Marx and Frederick Engels, 'Fictitious Splits in the International (1872)', in *Selected Works*, vol. 2, p. 285.
[11] Ernest Gellner, *Conditions of Liberty: Civil Society and Its Rivals* (London, 1994).

Gellner's study is important. It deserves careful attention, in no small measure because it is the best recent summary case for the fundamental contemporary relevance of the state–civil society perspective in the human sciences. Civil Society (the phrase is capitalized throughout by Gellner) 'is that set of diverse non-governmental institutions which is strong enough to counterbalance the state and, while not preventing the state from fulfilling its role of keeper of the peace and arbitrator between major interests, can nevertheless prevent it from dominating and atomizing the rest of society'.[12] He goes on powerfully to make the point that the contemporary popularity of the term is traceable to the fact that wherever it appears civil society, conceived as an *idealtyp*, is a zone of complexity, dynamism and choice, and that it therefore functions as the enemy of political despotism.

Gellner emphasizes that the opposition between civil society and political despotism was especially strong under the crisis-ridden totalitarian regimes of the Soviet type, or what he (a master of tropes) calls 'Caesaro-Papism-Mammonism'. Soviet totalitarianism achieved a 'near-total fusion of the political, ideological and economic hierarchies'. It was driven by the avowed aim of creating a new socialist man and woman emancipated from the ideology of possessive individualism, and from the facts of commodity fetishism and class exploitation. It manifestly failed to achieve these aims, Gellner insists. Instead, it cultivated cynical, obsequious subjects who were skilled at conniving double-talk. These 'individualists-without-opportunity' did not know or practise effective enterprise, not least because they were imprisoned in a world 'where it was barely possible – or literally not possible at all – to found a philatelic club without political supervision'.

* * *

Then came the *annus mirabilis* 1989. The largely non-violent revolutions that erupted in the central-eastern half of Europe in the autumn of that year put paid to this system. Not only did these 'velvet' revolutions represent a practical victory for

[12] Ibid., p. 5.

the forces of the emerging civil society that confronted the totalitarian regimes of the Brezhnevite or (in the case of emergent countries like Slovenia) Titoist type. These unfinished revolutions also vindicated the striking intellectual shift of emphasis towards the category of civil society. But why, we may ask again, did the downtrodden and humiliated – some of them in some countries, at least – find themselves attracted to the utopian language of civil society? Why did millions of people come bitterly to resent its absence, to feel its lack as an aching void? And why, after the revolutions, and elsewhere around the world, do so many people now argue for and about civil society?

Gellner arguably answers these important questions inadequately. That is unfortunate, because he misses the opportunity, for instance, to link the civil society perspective to the project of democratic politics. Gellner's positive characterization of civil society as a realm of freedom might have served to highlight its role as an indispensable condition of democracy: where there is no civil society, he might have argued, there cannot be speaking and interacting citizens with capacities to choose publicly their identities, decide their entitlements and honour their duties within a political-legal framework that secures peace among citizens, facilitates good government, promotes social justice and – above all – functions according to the principle that power, wherever it is exercised, must be publicly accountable. It is odd that Gellner does not express things in this way. He prefers instead to fall back upon the mid-nineteenth-century liberal argument that civil society has little to do with democracy. The latter is haphazardly defined by him in a strangely classical manner as 'a society which is the fruit of the will of its participants or members'.

Gellner prefers instead to couch his defence of civil society in terms of a theory of the unusual social tradition generated by the rise of modern industrial capitalism. We are the fruit of what we desire and endorse, he argues. Stirrings and strivings for civil society have become encoded within our modern historical tradition. *Conditions of Liberty* has an unfortunate habit of talking in such bad abstractions as 'we' – as if civil societies all spoke with one voice, which they manifestly do not – and as well pays too little attention to the uneven spatial and temporal distribution of the civil society traditions in which it is said 'we' are steeped.[13] *Conditions of Liberty* consequently tends to conflate different forms of civil society, which for instance can be more or less structured by xenophobia or racism or religion or homophobia or misogyny or violence or uneven patterns of market-generated wealth and income.[14] Gellner tries to sweep away such nuances with the bold thesis that civil society has become part of our make-up. We actually like it, and therefore have little or no desire to live under any form of state despotism or tradition-bound community. This desire is a complicated manifestation of the emergence of industrial capitalism. 'Civil Society . . . seems linked to our historical destiny', he writes. 'A return to stagnant traditional agrarian society is not possible; so, industrialism being our manifest destiny, we are thereby also committed to its social corollaries.' Gellner's point here is that civil society is best thought of as a functional offshoot of modernizing economies. That is why he chooses to speak of civil society in economistic terms. Civil society is seen as a type of social order in which 'the economy is separate from the polity', and in which 'the economy is not merely independent but actually dominant'. Gellner replies to Marxism's ridiculing of 'bourgeois' liberalism with a liberal taunt: 'Marxism made it a taunt that the bourgeois state was merely a kind of executive committee of the bourgeoisie: that this should have even become possible is perhaps mankind's greatest social achievement ever.'

Gellner supplements this claim about the (emergent) tradition of civil society driven by industrial capitalism with the closely related, structuralist argument that a civil society is a necessary condition of liberty. He reiterates the familiar point that civil society is not a suffocating segmentary community

---

[13] Jenö Szücs, *Les Trois Europes* (Paris, 1988).

[14] Compare my preliminary attempts to distinguish among more or less violence-ridden civil societies in *Reflections on Violence* (London and New York, 1996). Models of more or less market-dominated civil societies are sketched in *The Media and Democracy* (Cambridge, 1991), especially pp. 116–62.

ridden with customs and rituals and other forms of ascribed identity. Civil society is 'based on the separation of the polity from economic and social life' and 'the absence of domination of social life by the power-wielders'. It is exactly this spatial independence of civil society, its ability to act at a distance from political rulers, that enables the subjects of civil society to become self-moving, self-confident individuals. Not only do the complex and diverse patterns of life within civil society weaken essentialist notions of the human condition ('the inhabitant of Civil Society . . . is radically distinct from members of other kinds of society. He is not *man-as-such* [sic]', writes Gellner). Among the additional charms of civil society is the fact that its webs of networked activities and standards of excellence foster the illusion of equality of opportunity. Gellner here upends the old complaint about the disunity caused by civil society. 'Eternally shackled to a single fragment of the whole,' wrote Schiller in the famous sixth epistle of his *Aesthetische Briefe*, 'humanity develops into nothing but a fragment.'[15] Such disharmony, Gellner replies, is positive for civil society fosters the struggle for self-improvement. 'Civil Society . . . allows quite a lot of people to believe themselves to be at the top of the ladder, because there are so many independent ladders, and each person can think that the ladder on which he [sic] is well placed is the one that really matters.'

---

[15] Friedrich Schiller, *Werke, Nationalausgabe*, ed. L. Blumenthal and Benno von Wiese (Weimar, 1943–67), vol. 20, pp. 323–325.

Nationalism

The case for civil society presented by *Conditions of Liberty* is illustrative of what is to be avoided, since it falls in with the unfortunate company of Dr Pangloss by supposing, in opposition to the neo-Marxian and Islamist critics of civil society, that all that goes on within actually existing civil societies is for the best in the best of all possible worlds so far known to humanity. Civil society is treated as something of an idealized counter image of state institutions. It is the incarnation of social virtue in opposition to political vice. Civil society is the breeze of an approaching dawn. It is the realm of freedom contrasted with the realm of coercion. Civil society is pluralism, participation, purity, reflexivity. The state is conformity, directives, corruption, blind compulsion. Actually, Gellner's book reveals the pitfalls of liberal versions of the theory of civil society – and the intellectual and political dangers of complacently supposing that actually existing civil societies are havens of complexity and choice, that they are engines of righteousness, that they provide the natural habitat in which 'liberty' can and does flourish. *Conditions of Liberty* unfortunately leaves itself wide open to the flimsy objection, long ago put forcefully by Michel Foucault, that the discourse about civil society is weakened by 'a sort of Manichaeism that afflicts the notion of "state" with a pejorative connotation while idealizing "society" as a good, living, warm whole'.[1] To put

[1] Michel Foucault, *Politics, Philosophy, Culture: Interviews and Other Writings 1977–1984* (New York, 1988), pp. 167–8.

the point more constructively: the key problem with Gellner's account is that it fails to see the need permanently to develop new images of civil society. It wrongly supposes that civil societies are largely unencumbered by self-paralysing contradictions and dilemmas and, hence, that they are exceptions to Anaximander's Rule that all human orders, by virtue of their humanness, are permanently subject to being judged guilty for their injustices and to pay the corresponding penalties, according to the ordinances of time.

Gellner's neglect of the potentially contradictory relationship between national identity, nationalism, civil society and democracy is a pertinent example of this weakness within his account. His writings on nationalism are well known.[2] But their key suggestion that nationality is a complex offshoot of modern industrialization – that we moderns are compelled to harness our cultural identity to the economic, educational and territorial state bureaucracies which surround us – is both excessively functionalist and neglectful of some key political questions: What is the political significance of a nation? Do nations have a right to political self-determination? If so, does that mean that the national identity of citizens is best guaranteed by a system of civil society and democratic government, in which power is subject to open disputation and to the consent of the governed living within a carefully defined territory? And what of nationalism? Does it differ from national identity? Is it compatible with civil society and democracy? If not, can its growth be prevented, or at least controlled?

*   *   *

These questions concerning national self-determination and civil society are worth examining in some detail, and not only because of their crucial contemporary political relevance. They need pursuing in order to illustrate the kind of fresh and unsentimental rethinking of the inherited theory of civil society that is urgently required if the friends of civil society are to avoid falling into the trap of foolishly idealizing its capacity for pro-

---

[2] Ernest Gellner, *Nations and Nationalism* (Oxford, 1983). See also his *Encounters with Nationalism* (Oxford, 1994).

moting the freedom, equality and solidarity of citizens. The neglect of these questions in contemporary discussions of civil society is especially strange, considering that their roots run deep into early modern Europe. With the decline of the Carolingian Empire, a new sense of collective identity, national awareness, began to emerge as a powerful social force. This process of nation building was championed by sections of the nobility and the clergy, who used derivatives of the old Latin term *natio* to highlight their sharing of a common language and common historical experiences.[3] The 'nation' did not refer to the whole population of a region, but only to those classes which had developed a sense of identity based upon language and history, and had begun to act upon it. Nations in this cultural sense were seen as distinctive products of their own peculiar histories.

From the fifteenth century onwards, the term 'nation' was employed increasingly for *political* purposes. According to the classic definition of Diderot, a *nation* is 'une quantité considérable de peuple qui habite une certaine étendue de pays, renfermée dans de certaines limites, et qui obéit au même gouvernement'.[4] Here 'nation' described a people who shared certain common laws and political institutions of a given territory. This political conception of 'the nation' defined and included the *societas civilis* – those citizens who were entitled to participate in politics and to share in the exercise of sovereignty – and it had fundamental implications for the process of territorial state building. Struggles for participation in the state assumed the form of confrontations between the monarch and the privileged classes, which were often organized in a parliament. These classes frequently thought of themselves as advocates of 'the nation' in the political sense of the term. They insisted, in opposition to their monarch, that they were the representatives and defenders of 'national liberties' and 'national

---

[3] Helmut Beumann and W. Schroeder (eds), *Aspekte der Nationenbildung im Mittelalter* (Sigmaringen, 1978); Helmut Beumann, 'Zur Nationenbildung im Mittelalter', in Otto Dann (ed.), *Nationalismus in vorindustrieller Zeit* (Munich 1986), pp. 21–33; and Bernard Guenée, *L'Occident aux xive à xve siècles* (Paris, 1981), chapter 3.
[4] *Encyclopédie* (17 volumes, Paris, 1751–65), vol. 11, p. 36.

rights'.[5] If the sovereign monarch came from a different nation – as in the Netherlands during the war against Habsburg
Spain – then such claims were sharpened by another dimen-
sion: the struggle for privileged liberties was transformed into
a movement for national emancipation from foreign tyranny.[6]

During the century of Enlightenment, something dramatic
happened to the language of the nation. The struggle for
national identity was broadened and deepened to include
the non-privileged classes. Self-educated middle classes, arti-
sans, rural and urban labourers, and other social groups demanded inclusion in 'the nation', and this necessarily had
anti-aristocratic and anti-monarchic implications. From here
on, in principle, the nation included everybody, not just the
privileged classes; 'the people' and 'the nation' were supposed
to be identical. Thomas Paine's two-part *Rights of Man* (1791–
2), for its time the biggest-selling book ever in the history of
book publishing, was the most influential European attempt
to 'democratize' the theory of national identity in this way.[7]
Rights of Man sparked bitter public arguments about the merits of monarchies and republics, forced Paine into permanent
exile from his native England hunted by death threats, and
led to a general crackdown against 'Paineites', all for suggest-
ing that each nation is entitled to its own system of representative government.

Paine had first proposed this thesis during the American
Revolution and several of his eighteenth-century contempor-
aries – Vattel and Sieyés, for example – had explored, or were
exploring, the same theme. Paine's prose burned with the
drama of the French Revolution. Its bristling optimism also

---

[5] The example of the English Parliament during the Tudor period is analysed by G.R. Elton, 'English national self-consciousness and the Parliament
in the sixteenth century', in Otto Dann (ed.), *Nationalismus in vorindustrieller
Zeit* (Munich, 1986), pp. 73–82. The French case is considered in R. Bickart,
Les Parlements et la notion de souveraineté national (Paris, 1932).
[6] The case of the Netherlands is examined in Johan Huizinga, 'Patriotism
and Nationalism in European History', in *Men and Ideas: History, the
Middle Ages, the Renaissance* (New York, 1959), pp. 97–155.
[7] Thomas Paine, *Rights of Man: Part First* and *Rights of Man: Part Second*, in
Philip S. Foner (ed.), *The Complete Writings of Thomas Paine* (New York,
1945), pp. 243–458.

reflected the breakthroughs of the American Revolution: the declaration of the natural and civil rights of the sovereign people of a nation, including the right to resist unlawful government, and the establishment of a republican democracy on a wholly new federal basis. Paine spat at the court and government of George III and warned all other monarchic rulers that the outbreak of revolution in Europe heralded a new dawn for democratic principles. 'Monarchy is all a bubble, a mere court artifice to procure money', he wrote, although he admitted that the pompous power and money grubbing of monarchy still trapped the world in a cage of war and rumours of war. 'There are men in all countries', he continued, 'who get their living by war and by keeping up the quarrels of nations.' He nevertheless insisted, in the face of this trend, that citizens of all nations, united in their love of republican democracy, had a duty to expose the taxing hypocrisy, fraud and gun-running of monarchic despotisms, understood as aggressive governments accountable only to themselves. And he concluded that the struggle for representative government – for periodic elections, fixed-term legislatures, a universal franchise and freedom of assembly, the press and other civil liberties – required recognition of the right of each nation to determine its own destiny. In effect, Paine envisaged something like a holy global alliance of self-governing nations, working in harmony for the common good of humanity. 'What is government more than the management of the affairs of a nation?' he asked. 'It is not', he answered. 'Sovereignty as a matter of right, appertains to the nation only, and not to any individual; and a nation has at all times an inherent indefeasible right to abolish any form of government it finds inconvenient, and establish such as accords with its interest, disposition, and happiness.'[8]

* * *

Paine's thesis that the nation and territorial government should constitute an indivisible unity, and that the right of national self-determination is basic, subsequently enjoyed a

---

[8] *Rights of Man: Part First*, op. cit., p. 341.

long and healthy life. During the nineteenth century, the proportion of revolutionary situations involving a clearly defined natural component rose to well over half. Nineteenth-century Europe saw the emergence of two great powers (Germany and Italy) based on the principle of national self-determination, and the effective partition of a third (Austria-Hungary after the Compromise of 1867) on identical grounds. The same principle was at work in the two revolts of the Poles in support of their reconstitution as a nation-state, and in the formal recognition of a chain of lesser independent states claiming to represent their sovereign nations, from Luxembourg and Belgium in the west to the Ottoman successor states in south-eastern Europe (Bulgaria, Serbia, Greece, Romania).

During our own century, especially after the First World War, the principle of 'the right to national self-determination' proved popular with international lawyers, political philosophers, governments and their opponents, who supposed that if the individual members of a nation so will it, they are entitled to freedom from domination by other nations, and can therefore legitimately establish a sovereign state covering the territory in which they live, and where they constitute a majority of the population. From this perspective, which often implied a vision of a holy alliance of self-governing nations, the principle that citizens should govern themselves was identified with the principle that nations should determine their own destiny. In turn, this equation produced a convergence of meaning of the terms 'state' and 'nation'. 'State' and 'nation' came to be used interchangeably, as in such official expressions as 'League of Nations', the 'Commonwealth of Nations', the 'law of nations' or 'nation-state', and in the commonplace English language usage of the term 'national' to designate anything run or regulated by the state, such as national service, national health insurance or national debt. Such expressions reinforce the assumption, traceable to the eighteenth century, that there is no other way of defining the word 'nation' than as a territorial aggregate whose various parts recognize the authority of the same state, an assumption captured in Karl

Deutsch's famous definition of a nation as 'a people who have hold of a state'.[9]

The principle that nations should be represented within a territorially defined state echoes into our times. In the European region – to mention several examples – the birth of Solidarność and the defeat of martial law in Poland, the dramatic velvet revolution and velvet divorce in Czechoslovakia, the collapse of the Berlin Wall to the trumpet sounds of 'Wir sind ein Volk', the forcible break-up of Yugoslavia, and the successful struggle of the Demos government and its supporters to achieve Slovenian independence – none of this can be understood without reference to the doctrine of national self-determination. The same powerful dynamic worked to secure the collapse of the multinational Soviet Empire. The Soviet Union was an empire comprising a diversity of nations all subject to the political dominance of a Russian-dominated Communist Party which ensured for seven decades that the federal units of the Union had no meaningful political autonomy and that demands for 'national communism' would trigger a political crackdown, backed if necessary by military force.

This multinational empire harboured a self-paralysing contradiction. The Party insisted on subjects' conformity to its Russified definition of policies for securing 'socialism' – 'national communism' of the Czechoslovak type was outlawed – all the while governing through national cadres, promoting national cultures, encouraging education in the local language and even talking of eventual rapprochement (*sblizhenie*) and assimilation of nations (*slyanie*). From the Khrushchev period onwards, this contradiction not only fostered the growth of national *nomenklatura* who ran the republics, particularly in Transcaucasia and Central Asia, as fiefdoms controlled by Party 'mafias' rooted in circles of friends, kinship networks, and local and regional systems of patronage. It also stimulated, especially during the Gorbachev period, the growth of civil societies expressing themselves in a national idiom, protesting against Russification, enforced industrialization and ecological dam-

[9] Karl Deutsch, *Nationalism and Its Alternatives* (New York, 1969), p. 19.

age, and demanding 'democracy' and 'independence', thereby lunging with a dagger at the heart of the imperial system structured by the leading role of the Russian-centred Party.[10]

*   *   *

The collapse of the Soviet Empire under pressure from struggles for national self-determination adds empirical weight to the eighteenth-century thesis that a shared sense of national identity, in Hungary and the Russian Federation no less than in Scotland and Slovenia, is a basic precondition of the creation and strengthening of citizenship and political democracy. In each case, the appeal to the principle of a self-governing nation *feels* democratic since, after all, the appeal is to *all* who belong to the nation summoned into action. The presumption that there is an elective affinity between national self-determination and democracy is often reinforced by the sociological claim that a shared sense of national identity is essential to the formation and survival of a vibrant, confident civil society. The reason that is most often given in support of this claim is that national identity, understood as an ideal-type, is a particular form of collective identity in which people, despite their routine lack of physical contact, consider themselves bound together because they speak a language or a dialect of a common language; because they inhabit or are closely familiar with a defined territory, and experience its ecosystem with some affection; and because they share a variety of customs, including a measure of *mémoires involontaires* (Proust) – internalized memories of the historical past – which itself is consequently experienced in the present tense as pride in the nation's achievements and, frequently, as an obligation to feel ashamed of the nation's failing.[11]

[10] Klaus von Beyme, 'Social and Economic Conditions for Ethnic Strife in the Soviet Union', in Alastair McAuley (ed.), *Soviet Federalism, Nationalism and Economic Decentralisation* (Leicester and London, 1991), pp. 89–109; and Adam Michnik, 'Nationalism', *Social Research*, vol. 58, no. 4 (Winter 1991), pp. 757–63.

[11] The contours of national identity are well examined in Philip Schlesinger, 'On National Identity: Some conceptions and Misconceptions Criticized', *Social Science Information*, vol. 26, no. 2 (1987), pp. 219–64; Ernest Gellner,

National identity so defined is a specifically modern European invention. It is Europe's (Greek) gift to the world, and
its importance for a revised theory of civil society is that it can
infuse citizens with a sense of purposefulness, confidence and
dignity by encouraging them to feel 'at home'. It enables them
to decipher the signs of institutional and everyday life. The
activity of others – the food they prepare, the products they
manufacture, the songs they sing, the jokes they tell, the clothes
they wear, the looks on their faces, the words they speak – can
be mutually recognized and understood. That familiarity in
turn endows each individual with a measure of confidence to
speak and to act. Consequently, whatever is strange is not automatically feared; whatever diversity exists within the nation is more or less accepted as one of its constitutive features.
The borders between a national identity and its 'neighbouring' identities (of occupation, class, gender, religion, race, for
example) are vaguely defined and its security police and border guards are unreliable and tolerant.[12] There is even some
acceptance of the fact that members of the same nation can
legitimately disagree about the meaning and extent of their
nationhood. This tolerance of difference is possible precisely
because national identity equips members of a nation with a
sense of belonging and a security in themselves and in each
other: they can say 'we' and 'you' without feeling that their 'I',
their sense of self, is slipping from their possession.

Whenever citizens are denied access to a shared sense of
nationhood, they tend to experience the world as unfriendly
and alien – in the extreme case of enforced exile they experience the nasty, gnawing, self-pitying and self-destructive
Hauptweh described by Thomas Mann and others – and this
renders them less capable of living democratically. After all,
democratic regimes are the most demanding of political

Nations and Nationalism, op. cit. and Benedict Anderson, *Imagined Communities: Reflections on the Origin and Spread of Nationalism* (revised edition; London and New York, 1991).
[12] The spatial metaphor of boundaries is developed in Fredrik Barth,
'Ethnic Groups and Boundaries', in *Process and Form in Social Life: Selected
Essays of Fredrik Barth* (London, 1981), pp. 198–227.

systems. In contrast to all forms of heteronomous government, democracy comprises procedures for arriving at collective decisions within the institutionally separated but interlinked domains of civil society and state structures, by means of non-violent public controversies and power-sharing compromises based on the fullest possible and qualitatively best participation of interested parties.[13] At a minimum, democratic procedures include equal and universal adult suffrage within constituencies of various scope and size, majority rule and guarantees of minority rights, which together ensure that collective decisions are approved by a substantial number of those expected to make them. Democratic procedures must also include freedom from arbitrary arrest, respect for the rule of law among citizens and their representatives, and constitutional guarantees of freedom of communication and assembly and other civil and political liberties, which help ensure that those expected to decide or to elect those who decide can choose among real alternatives. And democracy further requires various governmental and non-governmental social policies (in fields such as health, education, child care and basic income provision) which prevent the market exchanges of civil society from becoming dominant and thereby ensure that citizens can live as free equals by enjoying their basic political and civil entitlements. Expressed differently, democracy requires the institutional division between a certain form of state and civil society. A democracy is an openly structured system of sociopolitical institutions which facilitate the flexible sharing and control of the exercise of power. It is a multilayered political and social mosaic in which political decision-makers at the local, regional, national and supranational levels are assigned the job of serving the *res publica*, while, for their part, citizens living within the nooks and crannies of civil society are obliged to exercise vigilance in preventing each other and their political rulers from abusing their powers and violating the spirit of the commonwealth.

[13] John Keane, *Democracy and Civil Society: On the Predicaments of European Socialism, the Prospects for Democracy and the Problem of Controlling Social and Political Power* (London and New York, 1988; 1998) and *The Media and Democracy* (Cambridge, 1991).

Although democracy in this sense does not require citizens to play the role of full-time political animals – too much democracy can kill off democracy – it is always difficult to generate or to sustain its momentum. That task is rendered even more arduous in contexts lacking civil society traditions which are home to the virtues of democratic self-government: prudence, common sense, self-reliance, courage, sensitivity to power, the knack of making and defending judgements in public, the ability to (self-) criticize and to accept criticism from others in turn, and the capacity to join with others in dignity and solidarity to resist the enervating miasma of fear. The last-mentioned quality is especially important in the democratic transformation of despotic regimes, when fear of power corrupts those who are subject to it and fear of losing power corrupts those who exercise it.

Shaking off fear is always a basic condition of democracy and it is normally assisted by citizens' shared sense of belonging to one or more ethical identities, national identity being among the most potent of these. Fearlessness is not a naturally occurring substance. It is a form of courage or 'grace under pressure' (Aung San Suu Kyi) developed wherever victims of political lies and bullying and violence make a personal effort to throw off personal corruption and to draw on their inner and outer resources to nurture the habit of refusing to let fear dictate their actions. Grace under pressure normally precedes and underpins attempts to institutionalize democracy. To be effective, it must be practised in small daily acts of resistance that in turn feed upon citizens' sense that they speak a common language and share a natural habitat and a variety of customs and historical experiences.

*   *   *

Consider the case of Poland, which well illustrates this point. At the end of the eighteenth century, following the partitions of 1772, 1793 and 1795, Poland was carved up by the Russian Empire, the Habsburg monarchy and the kingdom of Prussia. Its nobility (*szlachta*) responded by nurturing a distinctive national consciousness. During the nineteenth century, these Poles considered themselves (and were widely regarded) as fighters for the freedom of humanity, as a nation martyred in the cause of democratic liberty everywhere. To be Polish implied the ability to act gracefully under pressure, the refusal to be bullied and intimidated by power. The leader of the revolt of 1794, Tadeusz Kościuszko, was a hero to many late-eighteenth-century European democrats and his name was celebrated in America and even in Australia, whose highest mountain is named after him. The Polish legions organized by Henryk Dabrowski took as their slogan 'for our liberty and yours' (*za nasza i wasza wolność*) and Polish patriots played a prominent part in the 1848 revolutions in Hungary, Germany and Italy.

Today, the national identity crystallized in such experiences surprises and even perplexes some people who are not Polish. The Poles are sometimes seen as brash and crafty anarchists who have a deeply romantic soul traceable to poets such as Adam Mickiewicz, who viewed Poland as the Christ of Nations, crucified so that it could be resurrected and all other nations could be redeemed. Such arrogance was indeed evident in the Pilsudski episode of the 1920s. Traces of the same arrogance are also still evident in various parts of today's political spectrum in Poland, especially in the ongoing calls for a 'Catholic State of the Polish Nation'. But overall, the messianic fervour with which certain nineteenth-century Poles reacted to misfortune and oppression has considerably declined. A striking feature of Polish national identity during the past two decades is its embrace of the language of democratic freedom; as Adam Michnik remarked after the birth of Solidarność, the Polish struggle for civil society and political freedom against military dictatorship and foreign domination is often viewed as a synonym for the freedom of other human beings.[14]

* * *

Both the Polish example and the preceding analysis appear to confirm the eighteenth-century doctrine of national self-

[14] See my interview 'Towards a Civil Society: Hopes for Polish Democracy', op. cit.; and 'Jan Jozef Lipski, "Two Fatherlands – Two Patriotisms" ', *Survey*, vol. 26, no. 4 (Autumn 1982), pp. 159–75.

determination. They seem to imply that Paine and others were correct in thinking that the defence of 'the nation' and the struggle for an open civil society and political democracy against arrogant despotism are identical, that when the winds of national feeling blow, the people, like beautiful birds, grow wings and fly their way to a land of social and political independence. And yet the experience of the French Revolution, which inspired many accounts of the doctrine of national self-determination, including Paine's *Rights of Man*, casts doubt upon any such conclusion. For a time, the rise of Louis Napoleon from the tumult of the revolution seemed to reveal a political weakness specific to the French events. Only in our time, after the logic of the French Revolution has been broadly repeated in so many countries, has it become possible to discern the operation of a new aspect of modernity, the unfolding of a process in which the French Revolution proved to be a fundamental watershed. The revolution destroyed forever the faith in the divine and unchallengeable right of monarchs to govern, and it sparked a struggle against the privileged classes in the name of a sovereign nation of free and equal individuals. However, those acting in the name of the sovereign nation were ever more tempted to emphasize faithfulness to *la patrie*: that is, citizens' *obligations* to their state, itself the guarantor of the nation, itself said to be 'one and indivisible'. The motto of the *ancien régime*, 'Un roi, une foi, une loi' ('One king, one faith, one law') was replaced by 'La Nation, la loi, le roi' ('The Nation, the law, the king'). Thenceforward the Nation made the law which the king was responsible for implementing. And when the monarchy was abolished in August 1792, the Nation became the titular source of sovereignty. 'Vive la Nation!' cried the French soldiers one month later at Valmy, as they flung themselves into battle against the Prussian army. Everything which had been royal had now become national. The nation even had its own emblem, the tricoloured national flag, which replaced the white flag of the house of Bourbon. The new spirit of *nationalism* had surfaced. The struggle for national identity turned fundamentalist, bringing with it a lust for the power and glory of the nation-state which finally overwhelmed the democratic potential of the revolution. The first nationalist dictatorship of the modern world was born.

*   *   *

The formation of a despotic regime sustained by nationalist appeals to the nation was an utterly novel development – Europe's poisonous gift to itself and to the rest of the world.[15] Since that time, and despite its extraordinary global impact, the eighteenth-century doctrine of national self-determination has been subject to a smouldering crisis, whose contemporary resolution necessitates a fundamental rethinking of that doctrine, a more complex understanding of the relationship between civil society, national identity and nationalism, and greater clarity in turn about the nature of citizenship and democratic procedures.

Max Weber once defined democracy for the benefit of General Ludendorff, and with his approval, as a political system in which the people choose a leader who then says, 'Now shut your mouths and obey me.'[16] The impatience with ongoing public clashes of opinion and disagreement implied in this definition of democracy misses one of its quintessential features. Whenever applied to the spheres of civil society and state, or intermediary mechanisms like political parties and corporatist negotiations, democratic procedures tend to maximize the level of reversibility or 'biodegradability' of decision making. They invite dispute and encourage public dissatisfaction with currently existing conditions, even from time to time stirring up citizens to anger and direct action. Under enduring despotisms – Salazar's Portugal or Brezhnev's Russia – things are otherwise. Time appears to stand still. Individuals continue to be born, to mature, to work and to love, to play and to

---

[15] Jacques Godechot, *La Grande Nation* (2nd edition; Paris, 1983); Eric Hobsbawm, *Nations and Nationalism since 1780* (Cambridge and New York, 1990); Hugh Seton-Watson, *Nations and States: An Enquiry into the Origins of Nations and the Politics of Nationalism* (London, 1977); and Benedict Anderson, *Imagined Communities*, op. cit.

[16] Cited in Marianne Weber, *Max Weber: A Biography* (New York and London, 1975), p. 653.

quarrel, to have children and to die, and yet everything around them becomes motionless, petrified and repetitious. Political life becomes utterly boring.

In fully democratic systems, by contrast, everything is in perpetual motion. Endowed with liberties to criticize and to transform the distribution of power within and between state and civil institutions, citizens are catapulted into a state of permanent unease which they can cope with, grumble about, turn their backs on, but never fully escape. The unity of purpose and sense of community of pre-democratic societies snaps. There is difference, openness and constant competition among a plurality of power groups to produce and to control the definition of reality. Hence there are public scandals which unfold when publics learn about events that had been kept secret, exactly because if they had been made public ahead of time they could not have been carried out without public outcries. Under democratic conditions the world feels as if it is gripped by capaciousness and uncertainty about who does and should govern. Existing relations of power are treated (and understood) as contingent, as lacking transcendental guarantees of absolute certainty and hierarchical order, as merely a product of institutionally situated actors exercising power within and over their respective milieux.

It is this self-questioning, self-destabilizing quality of democratic regimes which not only provides opportunities for the advocates of national identity to take their case to a wider public. It also increases the magnetism of anti-democratic ideologies such as nationalism. Democratic conditions can severely test citizens' shared sense of the unreality of 'reality' and the chronic instability in the distribution of power, to the point where they may crave for the restoration of certainty about 'reality' by suppressing diversity, complexity and openness within and between the state and civil society. Democracies never reach a point of homeostatic equilibrium. They are dogged permanently by public disagreements about means and ends, by uncertainties, confusions and gaps within political programmes, and by hidden and open conflicts. All this, in turn, makes them prey to forms of post-prison psychosis (Havel), to morbid attempts to simplify matters, to put a stop to pluralism and to foist Unity and Order on to everybody and everything.

*   *   *

The events of the French Revolution revealed this dynamic for the first time, confirming the rule that, whenever believers in a nation assemble, they risk being seduced by the language and power fantasies of nationalism. The analytic distinction between national identity and nationalism – overlooked by many commentaries on the subject, including Eric Hobsbawm's *Nations and Nationalism since 1780* – is fundamental in this context.[17] Nationalism is often the child of democratic pluralism – both in the sense that the existence of open state institutions and a minimum of civil liberties, including freedom of communication, enables nationalists to organize and to propagate their nationalism, and also in the less obvious sense that democracy, even a taste of it, often breeds insecurity about power and sometimes fear and panic, and, hence, the yearning of some citizens to take refuge in sealed forms of life.

In the European region, nationalism is at present among the most virile and magnetic of these closed systems of life, or what I prefer to call ideologies.[18] Like other ideologies, nationalism is an upwardly mobile, power-hungry and potentially dominating form of language game which pretends to be universal. It supposes that the Nation is a biological fact, and that it is the principal form of life, all the while hiding its own particularity by masking its own conditions of production and by attempting to stifle the plurality of non-national and sub-national language games within the established civil society and state in which it thrives.

Nationalism is a scavenger. It feeds upon the pre-existing sense of nationhood within a given territory, transforming that shared national identity into a bizarre parody of its former

[17] See Johan Huizinga, 'Patriotism and Nationalism in European History', op. cit.
[18] John Keane, 'The Modern Democratic Revolution: Reflections on Lyotard's *The Postmodern Condition*', in Andrew Benjamin (ed.), *Judging Lyotard* (London and New York, 1992), pp. 81–98.

self. The famous remark of Albert Camus, that he loved his
nation too much to be a nationalist, correctly grasped that
nationalism is a pathological form of national identity. Nationalism tends (as Milorad Pavić points out in a different way
in *Dictionary of the Khazars*) to destroy its heterogeneity by
squeezing the nation into the Nation. Nationalism also takes
advantage of any democratizing trends by roaming hungrily
through civil society and the state, harassing other particular
language games, viewing them as competitors and enemies to
be banished or terrorized, injured or eaten alive, pretending
all the while that it is a universal language game whose valid-
ity is publicly unquestionable, and which therefore views itself as freed from the contingencies of historical time and space.

Nationalism has a fanatical core. Its boundaries are dotted
with border posts and border police charged with the task of
monitoring the domestic and foreign enemies of the Nation.
In contrast to national identity, whose boundaries are not fixed
and whose tolerance of difference and openness to other forms
of life is qualitatively greater, nationalism requires its adher-
ents to believe in themselves and to believe in the belief itself,
to believe that they are not alone, that they are members of a
community of believers known as the Nation, through which
they can achieve immortality by living their essential nature.
Nationalism requires them and their leader-representatives (as
Ernest Renan put it in *Qu'est-ce qu'une Nation?*) to participate in 'un plebiscite de tous les jours'. This level of ideological commitment ensures that nationalism is driven by a bovine
will to simplify things – by the kind of instruction issued by
Bismarck: 'Germans! Think with your blood!'

If democracy is a continuous struggle against simplification
of the world, then nationalism is a continuous struggle to undo
complexity, a will not to know certain matters, a chosen ignorance, not the ignorance of innocence. It thereby has a tendency to crash into the world, crushing or throttling everything
that crosses its path, to defend or to claim territory, and to
think of land as power and its native inhabitants as a 'single
fist' (Ayaz Mutalibov). Nationalism has nothing of the humil-
ity of national identity. Like the cavalier attitude of Jean-
Marie Le Pen towards the Holocaust, nationalism feels no

shame about the past or the present, for it supposes that only foreigners and 'enemies of the nation' are guilty. It revels in macho glory and fills the national memory with stories of noble ancestors, heroism and bravery in defeat. It feels itself invincible, waves the flag and, if necessary, eagerly bloodies its hands on its enemies.

At the heart of nationalism – and among the most peculiar features of its 'grammar' – is its simultaneous treatment of the Other as everything and nothing. Nationalists warn of the menace to their own way of life posed by the growing presence of aliens. The Other is seen as the knife at the throat of the Nation. Nationalists are panicky and driven by friend–foe calculations; they suffer from a judgement disorder that convinces them that the Other nation lives at its own expense. Nationalists are driven by the feeling that all nations are caught up in an animal struggle for survival, and that only the fittest survive. Many speeches of Jörg Haider of the FPÖ in Austria insinuate that 'East Europeans' are endangering the state, the constitution and democracy. Neo-Nazis in the new half of Germany shout 'Ausländer' raus!', liken Poles to hungry pigs, attribute shortages of bicycles to the Vietnamese and lack of food to the Jews, and accuse Turks of taking over German communities. French supporters of Jean-Marie Le Pen warn of the Arab 'invasion' of France – once likened by Le Pen himself to an invasion of starlings hungry for ripening French cherries. Lithuanian anti-Semites whisper the old stories about the Jews who once sacrificed Christian children and used their blood to make Passover bread, and recall the same blood libellous tales of Jewish grain merchants and millers who put glass in their flour to make Gentile women bleed when they kneaded their dough. Croatian nationalists denounce Serbians as Četniks or as Bolshevik butchers who murder their victims and mutilate their bodies; Serbian nationalists reciprocate by denouncing Croats as Ustaše fascists who are hellbent on eliminating the Serbian nation. Both curse Muslims as Islamicized Serbs or Croats, or as foreign invaders of a land in which they have in fact lived a variety of identities for five centuries.

Yet nationalism is not only fearful of the Other. It is also arrogant, confidently portraying the Other as inferior rubbish, as a worthless zero. The Other is seen as unworthy of respect or recognition because its smelly breath, strange food, unhygienic habits, loud and off-beat music, and incomprehensible babbling language places it outside and beneath Us. It follows that the Other has few if any entitlements, not even when it constitutes a majority or minority of the population resident in the vicinity of Our Nation. Wherever a member of the Nation is, as Radovan Karadzič once put it, there is the Nation. It is true (as Lenin emphasized) that the nationalism of a conquering nation should be distinguished from the nationalism of those whom it conquers, and that conquering nationalism always seems uglier and more culpable. It is also true that nationalism can be more or less militant, more or less hypocritical, and that its substantive themes can be highly variable, ranging from attachment to consumption and a treasured form of currency to boundary-altering forms of political separatism. Yet despite such variations and differences, nationalists suffer from a single-minded arrogance. 'Nationalism threatens not only bellicosity toward rivals but repression of internal difference.'[19] This arrogance leads nationalists to taunt and spit at the Other, to label them as wogs, *Scheiss* and *tapis*, to discriminate against them in institutional settings and on the streets, to prohibit the public use of minority languages ('linguicide'), or even, in the extreme case, to press for the expulsion of the Other for the purpose of creating a homogeneous territorial nation. Then nationalism is driven by a fanatic desire to purify a community of its bad elements, to weld together the pure by the emotions of hatred of the Other and guilt for the crimes that have been committed in common. In the extreme case, nationalism becomes 'a continuation of totalitarianism by other means'.[20]

This murderous *reductio ad absurdum* of nationalism surfaced on the southern fringes of Europe during and after World

[19] Craig Calhoun, 'Civil Society and the Public Sphere', *Public Culture*, no. 5 (1993), pp. 275–6.
[20] Dominique Colas, *Civil Society and Fanaticism: Conjoined Histories* (Stanford, 1997), p. xxvii.

War I, with the mass extirpation of Armenians from Turkey in 1915 and, after the crushing defeat of the Greek army by the Turks in Anatolia in 1922, the expulsion by Greece of some 400,000 Turks and a reciprocal expulsion by the Turks of perhaps 1.5 million destitute and panic-stricken Greeks from the lands of Asia Minor, where they had lived with others since the time of Homer.[21] The herding and murdering of nations was repeated by Stalin and by Hitler, who insisted on the elimination of the Jews and others, and offered forceful incentives for the transfer of South Tyrolians and other German-speaking peoples living outside the *Vaterland* to Germany itself. The same bizarre and bloody process lately reappeared in the armed defence of 'Serbian autonomous republics' and the military occupation by Serbia of Kosovo in former Yugoslavia. The Kosovo region proved to be the testing ground of Serbian expansionism. Its nationalist spokesmen, tossed between the horns of arrogance and fear common to all nationalists, attacked Albanian Kosovars as dirty, backward Muslims who are not a genuine Yugoslav nation (*nacija*) but a mere unimportant nationality (*nacionalnost*) of non-Slavs. At the same time, they viewed Kosovars as fanatical conquerors, and they consequently called for 'the severing of the right hand of all those who carry the green flag of Islam' (Vuk Drasković) in the historic cradle of the Serbian Nation, where King Lazar and his army were slaughtered while defending Christendom and civilization against the crescent and scimitar of all-conquering Islam. This same view of Muslims as worthless invaders subsequently tore Bosnia-Herzegovina to shreds. Innocent civilians were shot at. They were herded at gunpoint from their burning homes. They were summarily executed in nearby houses or, through a hail of mortar shells, marched in columns to railway sidings past rotting corpses to concentration camps, where they were raped or castrated, and then made to wait, with bulging eyes and lanternous faces, for the arrival of their own death.

*   *   *

[21] See Charles B. Eddy, *Greece and the Greek Refugees* (London, 1931), and C.A. Macartney, 'Refugees', in *Encyclopedia of the Social Sciences* (London, 1931), vol. 13, pp. 200–5.

Nationalism is evidently a serious and dirty business, in this case resulting in the forcible tearing apart of Yugoslavia and the destabilization of the whole Balkan region, with considerable ecological damage, economic ruin, psychic misery, and more than two-and-a-half million refugees and many thousands killed or wounded or psychologically damaged. How can destructive processes of this kind be explained?

Contrary to the most popular explanation, nationalism is not caused by the periodic re-emergence in the human breast of atavistic instincts of *Blut und Boden*. Such emphasis on the primordial roots of nationalism correctly pinpoints its deeply emotive dimensions, but, devoid of any historical understanding, it cannot account for why nationalism appears when and where it does. Furthermore, contemporary nationalism of the Serbian or French or English or Georgian variety is not primarily understandable in neo-Marxian terms as the political response either of a beleaguered or an expansionist bourgeoisie (Austro-Marxism) or of classes exploited by capitalist imperialism (Tom Nairn) or by the reckless, creative destruction of the global capitalist economy (Slavoj Žižek). Class domination, deindustrialization, unemployment and the formation of a new underclass of anxious citizens are indeed contemporary consequences of economies structured by commodity production and exchange, but they do not spontaneously provoke the growth of nationalism. For that to happen, there must be at least some elements of a pre-existing shared sense of national identity that is in turn capable of political manipulation and public deployment by power groups taking advantage of the openness and *déracinement* cultivated by actually existing civil societies and democratic mechanisms.

If nationalist tendencies are not entirely blameable upon capitalism then neither are they ultimately traceable to the operations of 'real socialism'. The ruling Communist Party bureaucracies of countries such as Romania, Hungary, Slovenia and Poland stimulated nationalist tendencies in their effort to legitimate their grip on power, but the conclusion that nationalism is a toxic product of communism is unwarranted. Nationalism (as the Magyar resistance to the Habsburg Empire and many other examples suggest) pre-dated the era of twentieth-century communism in power and, besides, in central and eastern Europe nationalism has emerged much more forcefully in the phase of post-communism.

Since the 'velvet revolutions' of 1989–91, the nationalist card has not only been played by communist parties and organizations struggling to retain their power – Milosević in Serbia, Kravchuk in the Ukraine, and Iliescu in Romania are examples. It has been used as frequently by the anti-communist opponents of the *ancien régime* – Gamsakhurdia in Georgia, Tudjman in Croatia, and Yeltsin in Russia – who in this respect share something of fundamental importance with their communist foes. Both groups have learnt that in the early stages of democratization, when anti-communists lack money and communists lack ideas and conviction, nationalism can warm hearts, change minds and win votes, encouraging individuals and groups within an emerging civil society to embrace a shock-absorbing identity that washes away their sense of futility, encourages 'solidarity of the culpable' (Šiklová) and gives them the feeling of protection against the ongoing liminality – the lawless disequilibrium and disorientation – produced by the first steps towards democracy.

What can be done about nationalism? The tightly coupled relationship between national identity, nationalism, civil society and political democracy does not warrant the extravagant conclusion that national identity, the 'raw material' of nationalism, is a pathological, outdated, hopefully declining force that in the meantime is best cold-shouldered by both observers and citizens, who from here on dedicate themselves to speaking many languages and living many different cultures; it also does not warrant the tragic deduction that the democratic project is somehow the root cause of nationalism, and that therefore the grip of nationalism can be broken only by abandoning democracy. Monist interpretations of nationalism (as of any other phenomenon examined by the human sciences) are inadequate precisely because of their blind one-sidedness. That is why the novel thesis presented here aims not to replace existing accounts of nationalism but to *complicate* our understanding of a force that continues to be of fundamental importance in the life and times of modern Europe.

*   *   *

Among the likely casualties of this new interpretation is the eighteenth-century thesis that the defence of national identity is a basic condition of democratic government, and the corresponding vision, championed by Woodrow Wilson, Mazzini and others, of a holy alliance of self-governing nations working in harmonious partnership for the common good of humanity. That vision is at the same time too simple and too dangerous. From the outset it was blind to the difference between national identity and nationalism, underestimated the anti-democratic potential of the struggle for national identity and failed to foresee the murderous *reductio ad absurdum* of nationalism, and for these three reasons alone it has today left behind a trail of confusion about the proper relationship between national identity, civil society and democratic institutions.

Such confusion cannot be undone by speculative arguments between those who conclude that 'nationalism is the ideology of the twenty-first century' (Conor Cruise O'Brien) and their opponents who rely on the equally broad-brushed conclusion that 'the Owl of Minerva is now hovering over nations and nationalism' (Hobsbawm). Such generalizations understate the uneven patterns of distribution of nationalism within the European region, simplify its multiple causes, and shortcircuit the normative and strategic problem of how to disarm nationalism. From the civil society perspective, there is an urgent need to stretch the limits of the contemporary political imagination, to think differently about the intertwined problems of nationalism, national identity and democracy, and to consider how the limits of democracy can be overcome in practice by inventing new institutional methods of preventing the growth of democracy's own poisonous fruit.

Solving the problem of nationalism by democratic means is possible, but not easy. The thesis sketched here is that, since democratic mechanisms (including civil society) facilitate the transformation of national identity into nationalism, democracy is best served by abandoning the doctrine of national self-determination and regarding a shared sense of national identity as a legitimate but *limited* form of life. This thesis contains a paradoxical corollary: national identity, an important support of civil society and other democratic institutions, is best preserved by restricting its scope in favour of *non-national* identities that reduce the probability of its transformation into anti-democratic nationalism.

*   *   *

In the European context it is now possible to envisage – by means of this thesis – a cluster of four interdependent mechanisms which together can curb the force of nationalism and at the same time guarantee citizens' access to their respective national identities:

(1)   The first of these remedies is to decentre the institutions of the territorial nation-state through the development of interlocking networks of democratically accountable subnational and supranational state institutions. Their combined effect, if rendered accountable to their citizens, would perhaps be to improve the effectiveness and legitimacy of territorial state institutions and, more pertinently, to complicate the lines of political power, thereby reducing the room for manoeuvre of single nation-states and frustrating the nationalist fantasy of politically securing nations through strong, sovereign states that are prepared in principle to launch war on their neighbours or to crush their domestic opponents in the name of national preservation or salvation.

In effect, this remedy involves renewing – but at the same time democratizing – the more complex patterns of political power typical of the late medieval and early modern periods. The modern process of European state building entailed the eclipse of numerous units of power – free cities, principalities, provinces, estates, manors and deliberative assemblies – such that the five hundred or so political units that dotted the region in 1500 were reduced to around twenty-five units in 1900. There are now signs of a reversal of this process of building centralized state institutions. One symptom of this 'scattering' of political power is the renewed interest in local government as a flexible forum for conducting local politics and competently administering local policies, partly in response to the declining effectiveness of macroeconomic management and the retreat of the national welfare state in western Europe.[22] The same decentring of the nation-state 'downwards and sideways' is evident in the vigorous development of regional ideas and regional power in areas such as Catalonia, Wallonia, Emilia-Romagna, Andalucia, Scotland and the Basque region. Especially striking is the rapid growth and competitive success of industrial regions comprising interdependent networks of firms caught up in a process of double convergence (Sabel). Large firms increasingly attempt to decentralize into looser networks of operating units, subsidiaries and subcontractors producing more specialized products through more flexible production methods. Meanwhile, small firms attempt to build themselves into the wider forms of loan finance, marketing facilities, research and development and other common services for which large firms were once renowned, and which are now provided increasingly at the regional level.[23]

Finally, the trend towards stronger local government and a *Europe des régions* has been supplemented by the accelerating growth of supranational political institutions, such as the European Parliament, the Council of Europe and the European Court of Justice. An earlier phase of experiments with intergovernmental negotiations and economic cooperation has been complemented by a process of treaty making and a drive to political, legal and monetary union; although still highly undemocratic and permanently controversial, this trend is likely to prove as consequential for the future political shape of Europe as the Congress of Vienna in 1814, the Treaty of Versailles in 1919 and the Yalta Summit in 1945.

Member states of the European Union are required on many issues to accept the *acquis communautaire*, the body of trea-

---

[22] Richard Batley and Gerry Stoker (eds), *Local Government in Europe: Trends and Developments* (London, 1991).

[23] See Charles Sabel, 'Flexible Specialisation and the Re-emergence of Regional Economies', in P. Hirst and J. Zeitlin (eds), *Reversing Industrial Decline? Industrial Structure and Policy in Britain and her Competitors* (Oxford, 1989), pp. 17–70.

ties, laws and directives which have been agreed by its makers; there is a relative shift away from policy making by consensus towards qualified majority voting; and a consequent
quickening pace of Euro-legislation in all policy fields. In 1970,
for example, the Council of Ministers, on which each member government has a representative, adopted 345 regulations,
decisions and directives (the three main types of Community
law); by 1987 that total had reached 623, and it has more
than doubled again since that time. From standards of central
heating and housing to the purity of beer and wine, the clean-
liness of beaches, the conditions of women's employment and
the development of a common currency, the populations of
the EU are increasingly touched and shaped by European political integration. Meanwhile, following the 1996 Maastricht
Treaty of Union, the European Union has become a three-
pillared structure, comprising the original European Communities – the ESCE, EAEC and EC – plus the newly founded
Common Foreign and Security Policy (CFSP) and cooperation in Home and Judicial Affairs (HJA). In fostering the stated
goal of 'creating an ever-closer union among the peoples of
Europe' (Article A), the Treaty of Union 'constitutionalizes'
the principle of the 'Union Citizen'. The combined effect of
such trends, including the proposed monetary union of existing and future member states, is to weaken and dissolve the
principle of national self-determination. Such trends arguably facilitate the birth of a post-national Europe, in the sense
that they greatly complicate and constrain the exercise of
power through existing territorial states, thus adding to the
pressure on nationalist movements, parties, governments and
leaders to recognize the fact and legitimacy of countervailing
political powers, even in such sensitive matters as 'national
economic policy' and the resolution of so-called 'national conflicts'.

(2)   The formulation and application of *internationally recognized* legal guarantees of national identity is a vital adjunct of
the breaking down of the principle of the sovereign nation-
state. Such formal guarantees were pioneered in the four
Geneva Conventions commencing in 1929 and expressed

forcefully in the Universal Declaration of the Rights of Man ratified by the United Nations in December 1948: 'Everyone is entitled to the rights and freedoms set forth in this declaration, without distinction of any kind, such as race, colour, sex, language, religion, political or other opinions, *national* or social *origin*, property, birth, or other status' (italics mine).

The Maastricht Treaty of Union arguably extends and refines this principle of guaranteeing citizens' entitlement to their national identity by means of international supervision, thereby departing from the Enlightenment maxim that all sovereignty appertains to the territorially bounded nation. In constitutionalizing the principle of citizenship of the Union, the Treaty adumbrates links with the European Convention of Human Rights, specifies certain entitlements of citizens within a common framework, and requires the member states of the Union to agree upon certain *transnational* political rights. The last provision includes the right of any citizen of any member state who is resident in another member state to vote and stand for office in local government and European elections. Other citizens' entitlements are specified: the right of freedom of information across state frontiers; the right to petition the European Parliament and to make use of new parliamentary ombudsmen; the right of inhabitants of regions collectively to influence common policies through the Committee of the Regions; and citizens' right to diplomatic and consular protection by any member state whenever they are travelling or living outside the Union.

There are evident weaknesses in these provisions. The social basis of citizens' rights – freedom of movement of capital, labour, goods and services – has led some to criticize the Treaty's definitions of citizenship as the citizen-as-worker, thus making it especially defective for women and other people who are not in conventional, full-time employment. Criticism has also been voiced of the ways in which the legal instruments and enforcement procedures hinder citizens' attempts to claim rights that are common across the Union. And it is said that the difficulties experienced by 'third country migrants' – Moroccans living in France and Turks resident in Germany, for example – replicate in a larger arena

the familiar exclusion of people without the right nationality.

These criticisms are justified, but nevertheless the citizenship provisions of the Treaty of Union have far-reaching implications for the subject of national identity and nationalism.
The citizenship of the Union principle supposes that governments have a primary obligation to respect the wishes of their
populations, but it does not fall back on the old premise that
each nation requires a sovereign state covering the territory in
which it lives. 'Where the sentiment of nationality exists in
any force', wrote J. S. Mill, 'there is a *prima facie* case for unit-
ing all the members of the nationality under the same government, and a government to themselves apart.' The Treaty of
Union spots a murderous difficulty lurking in this early modern doctrine of national self-determination: if the political
boundaries of the earth are to be fixed by the criterion of
nationhood then, since nations do not see eye to eye (why
otherwise have state borders?) and do not live in discrete geographic entities, there will be no end to boundary disputes.
Every border is seen as necessarily faulty and as capable of
improvement through the annexation of some outlying territory in which one's own nation is living; and since this annexation must normally be imposed by the conqueror upon
the conquered, the struggle for 'national autonomy' contains
the seeds of 'territorial cleansing', pushing and shoving, refugees, statelessness, pogroms and war. The Treaty of Union correctly understands that from here on there is to be no forcible
redrawing of existing nation-state boundaries, and that, in the
European context, uncivil wars sparked off by nationalist pressures, rather than war between homogeneous nation-states,
have become the major threat to regional stability.

The citizenship of the Union principle also reminds Europeans of the increasingly multinational character of their states.
Of course, most European states have always been multinational, but recently that fact has been accentuated by large-
scale migrations. The permanent entry into western Europe
of more than 15 million non-EU people during the past half-
century has ensured that mononational states no longer exist,
and that even the oldest and most culturally 'homogeneous'

of civil societies in countries or regions such as Spain, England, Portugal, France and Germany are now vertical mosaics of nationalities which do not humbly accept their position as satellites of the currently dominant national identity. The Treaty challenges the early modern assumption that national loyalties are exclusive, and that civil society and democracy are therefore possible only in a nationally homogeneous state.

The principle of 'transnational citizenship' (Bauböck) calls instead for a new compromise among nations *within* states. It sees that the peaceful and democratic functioning of European states and societies necessitates reliance upon supranational monitoring and enforcement mechanisms and – in accordance with what has been called Brugman's paradox – implies recognition of the new principle that the various nations of any single state are entitled to their nationhood, and thus to live differently, as free equals. The Treaty of Union 'depoliticizes' and 'deterritorializes' national identity. It recaptures something of the eighteenth-century view, championed by thinkers like Burke and Herder, that national identity is best understood as a cultural entity: that is, as an identity belonging to civil society, not the state. It sees national identity as a *civil* entitlement of citizens, the squeezing or attempted abolition of which, even when ostensibly pursued by states in the name either of higher forms of human solidarity or of protecting the 'core national identity' (Isaiah Berlin), serves only to trigger resentment, hatred and violence among national groupings.

(3) Of equal importance as a guarantor of national identity and democracy against nationalism is a factor that has been barely discussed in the literature on the subject: the development of a mosaic of different identities within a civil society wherein national identity is a legitimate, but only one identity among others. This third antidote to nationalism is as potentially effective as it is paradoxical. It presumes that the survival and flourishing of national identity within states is possible only within a self-organizing civil society, which, however, provides spaces for citizens to act upon *other* chosen or inherited identities, thus *limiting* the probable role of national iden-

tity in the overall operation of state and civil institutions and political parties, communications media and other intermediary bodies. The paradox bears a striking parallel to the question of religious tolerance: the practice of a particular religion in a multireligious society requires – if bigotry and bloodshed are to be avoided – the principle of freedom of religious worship, which in practice entails recognition of the legitimacy of *other* religions and, hence, the simultaneous need of institutional guarantees of the freedom *not* to be religious.[24] The same maxim ought to be carried over into matters of national identity, for it is clear that to model either state institutions or civil society solely on the principle of national identity means privileging one aspect of citizens' lives, devaluing others and contradicting the pluralism so vital for a democratic civil society, thus rendering those citizens' lives nation-centred and one-dimensional and, thus, susceptible to the rise of nationalism.

The straitjacketing effect of nation-centred politics in Croatia has been well described by Slavenka Drakulic: 'Nationalism has been forced on people like an ill-fitting shirt. You may feel that the sleeves are too short and the collar too tight. You might not like the colour, and the cloth may itch. But you wear it because there is no other. No one is allowed *not* to be Croatian.'[25] The converse of this point about the imperialism of nationalism is clear: an open, self-governing civil society protected by various tiers of state institutions requires the cultivation of a complex habitat of nested spaces. Within these spaces, citizens can protect themselves against the dangers of 'uprootedness' in a democracy by learning how to belong to a

[24] This logic of toleration had deeper roots. Dominique Colas, *Le Glaive et le fléau: Généalogie du fanatisme et de la société civile* (Paris, 1992), chapters 1–3, shows how the efforts of sixteenth-century Protestant thinkers like Philipp Melanchthon to rescue and defend the ideal of *societas civilis* as the antidote of religious fanaticism paved the way, intellectually speaking, for various arguments for tolerating (some) religious differences within the Earthly City of civil society. The earthly privileging of *societas civilis* also served unintentionally to fuel a dispute between the two swords, temporal and spiritual, that later fed into the eighteenth-century distinction between the state and a civil society containing a variety of different sects.
[25] Slavenka Drakulić, 'The Smothering Pull of Nationhood', *Yugofax* (31 October 1991), p. 3.

variety of organizations which enable them to put down roots, thereby preserving particular memories of the past, a measure of stability in the present, and particular expectations for the future. These spaces can further counteract nationalist pressures by helping citizens to overcome their own parochialism. Through their participation in the relatively local organizations of civil society, citizens find the most effective cure of their localism by learning about the wider world, coming to see that their sense of national identity – thinking and feeling themselves to be German, Irish, Turkish or Jamaican, or some hybrid combination of these – is not essentially superior to that of other nations, and that nationality is only one possible identity among others.

*   *   *

(4) Perhaps the most difficult-to-cultivate antidote to nationalism is the deterritorialization of national identity by means of an *international* civil society, in which citizens of various nationalities can intermingle, display at least a minimal sense of mutual understanding and respect, and generate a sense of solidarity, especially in times of crisis: for example, during natural disasters, economic collapse or political upheaval.[26]

During the second half of the eighteenth century, this friendship among citizens of various nations was called cosmopolitanism. Exposure to foreign contacts came in a variety of overlapping and sometimes contradictory ways: young men sent abroad to study; foreigners invited and welcomed as teachers; involvement in European wars which took 'nationals' elsewhere in Europe; increased travel among the 'respectable' classes and regular diplomatic relations with courts; expanding commerce; and the ever faster and wider circulation of foreign fashions in philosophy, letters, books and pamphlets, instruction, dress and social intercourse. A history of eighteenth-century cosmopolitanism has yet to be written, but it is clear that in the writings of Pietro Verri, Immanuel

---

[26] See the brief introductory remarks in Michael Walzer (ed.), *Toward a Global Civil Society* (Providence and London, 1995), pp. 2–4.

Kant, Thomas Paine and others the 'true cosmopolite' and the 'loyal patriot' were one and the same figure.[27] There was seen to be no contradiction between feeling oneself to be a citizen of the wider world – note the Greek roots of *kosmopolitēs* from *kosmos*, world and *politēs*, citizen – and wanting to enlighten and to transform that little corner of the European world where one had been born or had been brought by destiny to live, work, love and die. Early modern cosmopolitanism soon declined. Paine continued until his last breath to champion the cause of republican democracy around the world and Kant still looked at the history of the world *in weltbürgerlicher Absicht*, but these figures were among the last voices of a declining age. With the French Revolution the era of cosmopolitanism waned and into its place stepped nationalism, nation-state building and nation-state rivalry. Some continued to work for 'internationalism', guided by the principle that 'in proportion as the antagonism between classes within the nation vanishes, the hostility of one nation to another will come to an end' (Marx and Engels). Others converted their cosmopolitanism into the project of colonizing others. But slowly and surely the word *patriot* became charged with all the hatred and love of modern nationalism, while the word *cosmopolite* became the symbol of an ideal political unity that in practice could never be achieved.

A pressing theoretical and political question in today's Europe is whether a new form of the old cosmopolitanism is developing in tandem with the process of supranational political integration in the West and the attempted dismantling of totalitarian regimes in parts of central-eastern Europe. Is the growth of an international civil society in Europe possible

---

[27] The Italian case is examined in Franco Venturi, *Italy and the Enlightenment: Studies in a Cosmopolitan Century* (New York, 1972). See also Thomas J. Schlereth, *The Cosmopolitan Ideal in Enlightenment Thought: Its Form and Function in the Ideas of Franklin, Hume and Voltaire, 1694–1790* (Notre Dame and London, 1977); Eugen Lemberg, *Geschichte des Nationalismus in Europa* (Stuttgart, 1950), pp. 123–7; Joseph Texte, *Jean-Jacques Rousseau and the Cosmopolitan Spirit in Literature: A Study of the Literary Relations between France and England during the Eighteenth Century* (London and New York, 1899).

or actual? Raymond Aron is among those who have answered firmly in the negative: 'Rights and duties, which in Europe, as elsewhere, are interdependent, can hardly be called multi-national. In fact, they are quintessentially national . . . Though the European Community tends to grant all the citizens of its member states the same economic and social rights, there are no such animals as "European citizens". There are only French, German, or Italian citizens.'[28]

Aron's conclusion is not only based on the legal tautology that individuals can become citizens only because they belong to a sovereign state which is the sole guarantor of *ius soli* or *ius sanguinis*, upon which citizenship rights and duties are founded. Aron's conclusion has in any case been overtaken by events, in that it does not take account of the growth of multinational states and societies and the trend towards the definition of the rights of *European* citizenship, available to all who live within the European Union. These entitlements, examined by the 1996 Inter-Governmental Conference, provide further evidence that Europe – at least the three-pillared Europe of the European Union – is witnessing the slow, unplanned, blind and painful birth of a new species of political animal, *the European civilian*. This transnational civilian is not yet fully guaranteed in constitutional terms. Its 'informal' or semi-legal status renders it less than fully visible, ensures its strength as a normative ideal, and makes it vulnerable to countervailing trends. And yet the new European civilian can take advantage of an emerging European civil society comprising a *macédoine* of personal contacts, networks, conferences, political parties, social initiatives, trade unions, small businesses and large firms, friendships, and local and regional forums. Within this non-governmental habitat, individuals and groups of various nations and persuasions take advantage of new communications technologies – fax machines, answerphones, cheap flights, satellite broadcasting, email – which break down the apparently 'natural' barriers of geographic distance and state borders, increase the physical and cultural mobility of people,

---

[28] Raymond Aron, 'Is Multinational Citizenship Possible?', *Social Research*, Winter 1974, pp. 652–3.

and even simulate the possibility of being simultaneously in two or more places.

The new European civilians intermingle across frontiers for various purposes without making a cult of national origins, national identity and 'foreigners'. These civilians see and feel the importance of the *metaxu* (Simone Weil). They value nests, such as national identity, in which citizens are warmed and nourished and gain confidence in themselves. Yet they also recognize difference as a right and a duty for everybody. These new civilians maintain that, in the contemporary world, identity is more a matter of politics and choice than fate. They have an allergic reaction to nationalism and deep empathy for people suffering discrimination or enforced exile from their cherished nations or territories. They are humble about their own national identity, interested in others, concerned for their well-being, and consequently unwilling to indulge the feelings of revenge and narcissistic satisfaction characteristic of nationalists. European civilians are late modern cosmopolitans.

*   *   *

No doubt the internationalization of civil society is destroyed by nationalism and genocidal war, as in south-central Europe, where for many people daily life is now a non-citizens' hell of expulsion, terror, homelessness, and the fear and pain produced by bloodshed. There can be no doubt as well that, when all other methods have failed, violent nationalism must be checked by peace-making violence, whose means (von Clausewitz reminded us) should be used neither timidly nor (from a civil society perspective) recklessly. The social exchanges among a plurality of civilians within the European region can also be squeezed or suffocated by the power of transnational corporations seeking to coordinate their national markets, to trim and discipline their workforces, and to dominate European social life through profit-driven matrix management and marketing. It is also true that xenophobes and other anti-democratic forces are taking advantage of the new European habitat. Nevertheless the long-term growth of European-wide exchanges among civilians whose social and political views are predominantly pluralist and democratic is among the most remarkable – and least remarked on – features of contemporary Europe. Within these exchanges, there are few traces of Marxian class struggle politics and nineteenth-century dreams of abolishing state institutions, and nationalism is considered an anathema. Instead, there is an underlying belief that Europe from the Atlantic to the Urals, but perhaps even the world beyond, should become a coat of many colours, a region marked by a precarious, non-violent yet permanently contested balance between governors and civilians.

Sometimes this new European civil society erupts dramatically, as in the widespread popular desire to 'return to Europe' expressed during the velvet revolutions of 1989–91. At other times, it is acknowledged and expressed through legally codified references to the principle of citizenship rights and duties across frontiers (as in the Maastricht Treaty of Union and in the so-called 'Europe Agreements' that offer full membership in the EU to neighbouring states that respect and protect, among other things, their populations of minorities). But, most often, the formation of a European civil society is an undramatic, nearly invisible process that seems unworthy of the attention of journalists, intellectuals, politicians and policy makers. It clearly requires detailed investigation, and for this purpose the new civil society perspective that is currently being developed in Europe and elsewhere would seem to be well suited. The task is urgent, for could it be that this new European civil society, providing that it is not stillborn and that it is nurtured with adequate funding and legal and political guarantees, will prove to be among the best antidotes yet invented to the perils of nationalism and the poisonous fruits of democracy?

Uncivil society

The emerging consensus that civil society is a realm of freedom correctly highlights its basic value as a condition of democracy: where there is no civil society there cannot be citizens with capacities to choose their identities, entitlements and duties within a political-legal framework. Yet conservative critics of contemporary civil society have objected – powerfully, in preaching prose – that actually existing civil societies tend to destroy the civility upon which their character as a *civil* society depends. According to Edward Shils, the best-known exponent of this view, a civil society requires generous amounts of civility, understood as 'a solicitude for the interest of the whole society, a concern for the common good'. Especially under conditions of conflict, Shils argues, civil societies require for their stability 'the civil person', a publicly spirited creature, evidently masculine, who 'thinks primarily of the civil society as the object of his obligations, not of the members of his family, or his village, or his party, or his ethnic group, or his social class, or his occupation'. The civil person is equipped with 'good manners' that express deference and respect for others. 'Good manners are like uniforms and discipline which hide slovenliness, poor taste and unpleasing eccentricity', writes Shils, in the same breath as he laments the contemporary degradation of morals and manners. Greedy expectations of government, the breakdown of social authority, the growing consumption of narcotics, the practice of homosexuality, the growth of a lawless *lumpenproletariat*, strikes by public sector workers: such trends threaten to undermine civil societies and plunge them into rudeness, incivility and violence.[1]

Numerous objections can and should be lodged against this line of argument, whose moralizing, potentially authoritarian tone barely conceals the fact that it is an elaborate tautology redolent of a premodern understanding of civil society as a lawful and ordered political community. Shils and other conservative critics of civil society nevertheless have a point: today's friends of civil society have a bad habit of idealizing its untrammelled promotion of citizens' freedom, thereby overlooking what elsewhere I have termed the problem of incivility, the extreme case of which is an *uncivil society*.[2] The term 'uncivil society' is admittedly strange sounding, maladroit, at worst a malapropism, at best an anachronism, or so it seems. English-language dictionaries tell us that the word 'uncivility' is now virtually obsolete; that the sixteenth-century adjective 'uncivil' refers to behaviour which is 'contrary to civil well-being' or 'barbarous', 'unrefined', 'indecorous', 'improper', 'unmannerly' and 'impolite'. It was in this sense that country folk spoke of 'bad and uncivill Husbandry' (1632) or Shakespeare instructed one of his characters to command: 'Ruffian: let goe that rude uncivill touch'.

These observations about uncivility echoed the much older principle of civility elaborated in sixteenth-century Italian courts and seventeenth-century Parisian salons. According to this positive principle, the everyday interactions of men may, in such matters as commerce and love, not only be freed from the threat of violence – from incivility – but also become a source of pleasure. The natural potential for aggression among individuals and groups may be overcome by artificial conventions, such as refined speech, polite manners, effeminate styles of dress (wigs with long curls, jewels, ribbons, sinuously high-heeled pumps), all of which serve to distance individuals from uncivil habits variously dubbed rustic, crude, rude or unpolished. During this period, the French verb *civiliser* was used to name this process. *Civiliser* is 'to bring to civility, to make manners mild and civil'

[1] Edward Shils, 'Civility and Civil Society', in Edward C. Banfield (ed.), *Civility and Citizenship in Liberal Democratic Societies* (New York, 1992), pp. 1–15.
[2] John Keane, *Reflections on Violence* (London and New York, 1996).

under 'good government' and 'good laws'.[3] Mirabeau's *L'Ami des hommes ou Traité de la population* (1756), the first French text to use the new-fangled word *civilisation*, added that those who enjoyed a reputation for civility were considered exemplars of 'confraternity' or *sociabilité*; they were 'polished' men whose hearts had been softened, deflected from the temptations of taking violent revenge against others.

* * *

There was by no means general agreement in this period that the contemporary struggle against uncivility was a good thing. The invention of civility as an antidote to uncivility was synonymous with controversy. There were, for example, abundant complaints about the hypocrisy of civility, in particular because of the ways in which it served as a mask for the conniving egoism and violence of men with a reputation for refined manners. Mahatma Gandhi's famous remark that the idea of British civilization would be a good one stands towards the end of a long line of complaints of this sort, of which Jean-Jacques Rousseau's sarcastic, savage attack on Hobbes and modern civil society is among the most famous:

> I open the books on Right and on ethics; I listen to the professors and jurists; and, my mind full of their seductive doctrines, I admire the peace and justice established by the civil order; I bless the wisdom of our political institutions and, knowing myself a citizen, cease to lament I am a man. Thoroughly instructed as to my duties and my happiness, I close the book, step out of the lecture room, and look around me. I see wretched nations groaning beneath a yoke of iron. I see mankind ground down by a handful of oppressors. I see a famished mob, worn down by sufferings and famine, while the rich drink the blood and tears of their victims at their ease. I see on every side the strong armed with the terrible powers of the Law against the weak.[4]

[3] See Edmond Huguet, *Dictionnaire de la langue française du seizième siècle* (Paris, 1925), vol. 2, p. 302.
[4] Jean-Jacques Rousseau, 'Fragments of an Essay on the State of War' (written circa 1752), in *A Lasting Peace through the Federation of Europe and the State of War* (London 1917), pp. 124–5.

There were also attempts – well illustrated by Jonathan Swift's later questioning of English civility in defence of Irish independence[5] – to turn the tables on the powerful by emphasizing that their civility was the ally of arrogance, that it had the unintended effect of producing and reproducing incivility among the powerless, the key implication being that the powerful must somehow change their ways and let the 'uncivilized' find their own path to civility.

Despite such reservations and qualifications, the threat (and fear) of violence always seems to have been lurking behind the concern with civility. Uncivility was the ghost that permanently haunted civil society. In this respect, civilization was normally understood as a project charged with resolving the permanent problem of discharging, defusing and sublimating violence; uncivility was the permanent enemy of civil society. Civilization therefore denoted an ongoing historical process, in which civility, a static term, was both the aim and the outcome of the transformation of uncivil into civil behaviour. From this thesis it was merely a short step to the thought that the civilizing process was a march through stages of gradually increasing perfection. During the eighteenth century, the word 'civilization' connotes both a fundamental process of history and the end result of that process, in which the distinction between the advances of present-day civilization and the actual or hypothetical primitive primordial state (called variously nature, barbarism, rudeness or savagery) becomes ever clearer. The privileged classes of Europe represent themselves as treading a path stretching from primitive barbarism through the present condition of humanity to perfection through education and refinement.

The journey towards civilization is seen to be a slow but steady elimination of violence from human affairs, as Adam Ferguson, influenced by lectures delivered by Adam Smith in 1752, emphasized when first using the word 'civilization' in English. The process of civilization is described as progress from rudeness to refinement, in which the contemporary 'civil society' is understood as a 'polished' and 'refined' form of

---

[5] John Keane, *Reflections on Violence*, op. cit., pp. 15–17, 19.

society with 'regular government and political subordination'. Ferguson emphasized that 'the epithets of civilized or of polished' properly refer to 'modern nations', which differ from 'barbarous or rude' nations principally because of their discretionary use of violence. In barbarous nations, Ferguson insisted, 'quarrelling had no rules but the immediate dictates of passion, which ended in words of reproach, in violence, and blows'. Tides of violence flooded the field of government as well. 'When they took arms in the divisions of faction, the prevailing party supported itself by expelling their opponents, by proscriptions, and bloodshed. The usurper endeavoured to maintain his station by the most violent and prompt executions. He was opposed, in his turn, by conspiracies and assassinations, in which the most respectable citizens were ready to use the dagger.' Barbarous nations were equally rude in the conduct of war. 'Cities were razed, or inslaved; the captive sold, mutilated, or condemned to die.' By contrast, Ferguson observed, civilized or polished nations had gone some way in extruding crudely violent scenes from the stage of contemporary life. 'We have improved on the laws of war, and on the lenitives which have been devised to soften its rigours,' wrote Ferguson. 'We have mingled politeness with the use of the sword; we have learned to make war under the stipulations of treaties and cartels, and trust to the faith of an enemy whose ruin we meditate.' Civilized societies are guided by the principle of 'employing of force, only for the obtaining of justice, and for the preservation of national rights.'[6]

* * *

Among the weaknesses of this type of eighteenth-century interpretation of the problem of violence and civil society is its secret commitment to an evolutionary or teleological understanding of history as a process of transformation from 'rude' societies to 'civilized' societies. Ferguson himself worried about

---

[6] Adam Ferguson, *An Essay on the History of Civil Society* (Edinburgh 1767); especially part 1, section 4 ('Of the Principles of War and Dissension'), pp. 29–37; part 2 ('Of the History of Rude Nations'), pp. 112–64; and part 3, section 6 ('Of Civil Liberty'), pp. 236–56.

the possible relapse into barbarism, but the general framework of his study stands firmly on the assumption that modern times differ from and are superior to previous eras of rudeness because violence is potentially removable from significant areas of life. The evolutionary assumption is explicit in the works of other Scottish colleagues of Ferguson – such as James Dunbar's *Essays on the History of Mankind in Rude and Cultivated Ages* (1780) and John Logan's *Elements of the Philosophy of History* (1781) – who treat of violence as the antithesis of civil society and assume, optimistically, that it is on the wane in modern civil societies.

This unexplained optimism is of interest and consequence, since precisely the same premise is invisibly at work in most latter-day theorizations of civil society. I am convinced that this premise is rendered both questionable and undesirable by the terrible crimes of state violence committed throughout the twentieth century, some of which are detailed in my *Reflections on Violence*. The early modern presumption that violence is on the wane is also contradicted by the fact that it serves to distract our attention from three other basic facts of the long century of violence now drawing to a close: the chronic persistence of violence within all extant civil societies; the (not unrelated) permanent possibility that civil societies can and do regress into uncivil societies; and the (again related) long-term growth, for the first time on any scale, of a new *civilizing politics* aimed at publicizing and reducing the incidence of such disparate phenomena as murder and rape, genocide and nuclear war, the violence of disciplinary institutions, cruelty to animals, child abuse and capital punishment.

* * *

Within the twentieth-century social sciences, Norbert Elias did more than anybody to stimulate awareness of the first of these points, upon which I want mainly to concentrate. Elias's discussion of the strengths – and weaknesses – of the so-called civilizing process represents a pathbreaking attempt to counter the post-nineteenth century's loss of interest in and neglect of the topic of civility, and his effort, which is comparable in scope and intention with the older work of Rondelet,

Tocqueville and others,[7] is of vital importance to a theoriza-
tion of violence and civil societies.

His *Über den Prozess der Zivilisation* (1939) proposed that
from the sixteenth century onwards, particularly in the upper-
class circles of the courtoisie, social standards of conduct
and sentiment began to change drastically. Codes of conduct
became stricter, more differentiated and all-embracing, but
also more even, more temperate, banishing excesses of self-
castigation as well as of self-indulgence. Spontaneous behaviour was repressed; men who once ate from the same dish or
drank from the same cup or spat in each other's presence were
separated by a new wall of restraint and embarrassment at the
bodily functions of others; physical impulses (such as farting,
defecating and urinating) were checked by self-imposed pro-
hibitions and subjected to new rules of 'privacy'; prudery came
to surround wedding ceremonies, prostitution and discussions
of sexual matters; language became more delicate. Even death
itself became an embarrassment to the living. To express pleasure in violence, whether in mutilating one's opponents in
battle or in burning cats alive (an annual ceremony in Paris),
came to be regarded as rude and repulsive. Elias shows that
this transformation was closely related to the process of state
formation, particularly the subjection of the warrior classes to
stricter control and the 'courtization' of the nobles. The whole
process found its expression in a new term launched by
Erasmus of Rotterdam, the term 'civility', which later gave
rise to the verb 'to civilize', both of which were soon used in
many other countries as a symbol of the new struggle to refine and polish manners.

Elias argues that the civilizing process, which he does not
understand as synonymous with Europe or the West, is best
understood as a fragile historical episode linking the medieval
and contemporary modern worlds. Elias criticizes the tendency

---

[7] See C. Haroche, 'La Civilité et la politesse – des objets négligés de la
sociologie politique', *Cahiers internationaux de sociologie*, vol. 94 (1993),
pp. 97–120. The key work of Norbert Elias referred to here is *Über den
Prozess der Zivilisation: Soziogenetische und psychogenetische Untersuchungen*,
2 volumes, (Basel, 1939).

to use the term normatively, as if it were synonymous with the triumphs and achievements of modern Europe in the wider world. He comments:

> In 1798, as Napoleon sets off for Egypt, he shouts to his troops: 'Soldiers, you are undertaking a conquest with incalculable consequences for civilization.' Unlike the situation when the concept was formed, nations from here on consider the process of civilization as completed within their own societies; they see themselves as bearers of an existing or finished civilization to others, as standard-bearers of civilization in foreign lands. Of the whole preceding process of civilization nothing remains in their consciousness except a vague residue. Its impact is understood simply as an expression of their own higher gifts; the fact that, and the question of how, during the course of many centuries, their own civilized behaviour has been formed is of no interest.[8]

Elias correctly warns against this amnesia and its pompous political consequences. His warning could have more sting if it were tougher on the superiority complex of the European mode of civilization, for instance, or if it adopted a more rigorously sceptical attitude towards certain apparent civilizing trends. Elias's work contains something of an implicitly progressive view of the growth of modern patterns of civility, symptomatic of which is his general neglect of the ways (outlined by Foucault and others) in which the behavioural codes of a civilizing process may check the process of democratization of power and redeploy, sanitize and camouflage disciplinary and other violence without necessarily diminishing it. The nineteenth-century reduction of capital offences and the abolition of public hangings in 1868 in England, for example, can hardly be attributed to the growing practical triumph of liberal civility. Prosecutions and capital convictions had risen so dramatically by the early nineteenth century that by the 1830s more than 90 per cent of death sentences were not carried out lest the English landscape be clogged with gibbets, and not because of mounting humanitarian sympathy for the

---

[8] Elias, *Über den Prozess der Zivilisation*, op. cit., vol. 1, p. 63.

condemned. Similarly, the privatization of hangings, from the abolition of the Tyburn procession in 1783 to the dismantling of scaffolds inside prison walls in 1868, had little to do with a principled commitment to civility. The transfer of executions indoors, the hiding away of violence from the public eye, was sometimes seen by its advocates as a means of dampening public attacks on the whole dirty business of capital punishment. Hanging arguably also became more cruel, since felons were denied the active sympathy formerly extended to them by onlookers. Those whose hourglasses had been turned for the last time were now left to face death alone, in the hope – pious Anglicans calculated – that their sinful souls would repent.[9]

Elias nevertheless remains adamant: those Europeans who consider themselves the bearers of civilization resemble a tiny, courtly, aristocratic upper class lording over the rest of the world, an enclave falsely proud of their achievements, despite clear evidence that other civilizations – I shall not elaborate this point – have long enjoyed sophisticated methods of pacification and despite the fact, Elias adds, that the originally European mode of civilization is potentially self-paralysing. This emphasis upon the self-destructive limits of the civilizing process is particularly important because it highlights an exogenous source of incivility in civil societies. Elias's thesis can be put briefly: the modern civilizing process is directly related to the formation and growth of states seeking to disarm competitor power groups and thereby to monopolize the means of violence over a given territory and its inhabitants. The creation of the modern state – an impersonal, abstract entity that stands above and is distinct from both the government of the day and the governed – is synonymous with the erection of a sovereign and therefore indivisible power apparatus, the *defensor pacis* as Marsilius of Padova called it, that puts an end to social violence by wielding a monopoly of armed

---

[9] Michel Foucault, *Discipline and Punish: The Birth of the Prison* (London, 1975); V.A.C. Gatrell, *The Hanging Tree: Execution and the English People, 1770–1868* (Oxford, 1994); John F. Kasson, *Rudeness and Civility* (New York, 1990).

force over a population that enjoys freedom from everyday violence precisely because it agrees, more or less, to regard the state's monopoly of violence as legalized violence.

Such concentrations of the physical means of violence, which are normally controlled and managed by governments, backed up by the military and police as their executive organs, are, like so many other human inventions, highly equivocal. According to Elias, just as the taming of fire favoured progress in the cooking of food as well as the barbarian burning down of huts and houses, so the invention of states that exercise a monopoly of physical violence is an equally ambiguous innovation. States are positively dangerous instruments of pacification. On the one hand, within their given territories, they are peace-enforcing and peace-keeping agencies. The peace enjoyed by political subjects assumes the form of state-controlled and legalized violence, which releases individuals and groups from the hellish reality (in Hobbes's famous words) of 'continuall feare, and danger of violent death; And the life of man, solitary, poore, nasty, brutish, and short'. The exercise of violence consequently becomes, at least in principle, predictable and controllable. And yet, on the other hand, the modern process of state-secured pacification is not extended to the relationships among states, which, despite interstate negotiations, diplomacy and peace agreements, continue to be caught up in a *bellum omnium contra omnes*. The modern state is too civil by half. 'As in every system of balances with mounting competition and without a central monopoly, the powerful states forming the primary axes of tensions within the system force each other in an incessant spiral to extend and strengthen their power position.'[10] That means that war, whose essence is violence, the sparing use of which under battle conditions is imbecility, constantly threatens both particular states' monopoly of the means of violence (in that they can be defeated militarily by their enemies abroad or by civilian unrest at home) and the non-violent civil conditions enjoyed by their subjects. Elias's point is that the power of deploying the means of violence in the hands of a few and for

[10] Norbert Elias, *Über den Prozess der Zivilisation*, op. cit., vol. 2, p. 435.

the benefit of certain small groups can be used to make war on other states and their populations. War and rumours of war are omnipresent conditions of the civilizing process.

Those who enjoy a monopoly of the means of violence can also turn their life-threatening power against their own subject populations. Rousseau's remark that 'the whole life of kings, or of those on whom they shuffle off their duties, is devoted solely to two objects: to extend their rule beyond their frontiers and to make it more absolute within them'[11] applies to the whole of the modern period of states and state building. While premodern political systems normally attempted to ensure the obedience of their subjects and extract from them as much wealth as possible, they frequently lacked the resources for pulverizing and dominating the societies they attempted to control. They consequently resorted to the paradoxical strategy of allowing local communities and whole regions both to administer themselves and to supply money, produce or corvée labour, on pain of punishment. The modern state, by contrast, functions as an instrument of domination with concentrated armed force at its centre. It does so because at an earlier point in its history it disarmed autonomous feudal lords, communal militias, mercenaries, pirates and duelling aristocrats. The modern state is therefore potentially more terrible in its effects than premodern political systems. Its monopoly of the means of violence, as Hobbes remarked, places its subjects permanently under a cloud of threatened violence.

* * *

Elias is right to observe that state violence can and has often destroyed civility, leaving in its wake social relations riddled with incivility: violence, insecurity, aggravated conflict, old scores to be settled tomorrow or the day after. Dozens of contemporary societies around the world are currently suffering such symptoms, but there are scores of earlier recorded cases of overly strong

---

[11] Jean-Jacques Rousseau, 'A Lasting Peace through the Federation of Europe' (1756), in *A Lasting Peace through the Federation of Europe and the State of War*, op. cit., p. 95.

and expansionist centralized states undercutting the ability of subjects to organize themselves into non-violent, intermediary associations. From the time of the first wars linked to the state-building process in the Italian Renaissance and the violent destruction of religious groupings like the Huguenots by the French monarchy in the sixteenth and seventeenth centuries, violent rulers have gutted their respective societies and robbed populations of their capacity for peaceful self-organization except for kinship groups or state-sponsored organizations. Elias himself highlights this state production of barbarism in a chilling account of the Freikorps revenges in the Baltic area after Versailles. Pressured by entente and the peace treaty, the Berlin government ordered the withdrawal of German troops from the Baltic region. Many resentful Freikorps refused. They stayed and fought on, not against the Red Army, which had already retreated, but against reorganized Estonian and Latvian troops backed by British warships. The barbarism that ensued is illustrated by Elias with a citation from the diary of a Freikorps officer:

We fired into surprised crowds, and raged and shot and struck and hunted. We drove the Latvians across the fields like rabbits and set fire to every house and blasted every bridge to dust and cut every telegraph pole. We threw the corpses into the wells and threw in hand grenades. We killed whoever we captured, we burned whatever would burn. We saw red, we no longer had any human feelings in our hearts. Wherever we had camped, the ground groaned under our destruction. Where we had stormed, where formerly houses had stood, there now lay rubble, ashes, and glimmering beams, like abscesses in the bare fields. A huge trail of smoke marked our paths. We had ignited a huge pile of wood, which burned more than dead matter. On it burned our hopes, our desires: the bourgeois tablets, the laws and values of the civilised world, everything that we had dragged along with us as moth-eaten rubbish, the values and faith in the things and ideas of the time that had abandoned us. We pulled back, boasting, exhilarated, loaded with booty.[12]

[12] Norbert Elias, 'Violence and Civilization: The State Monopoly of Physical Violence and Its Infringement', in John Keane (ed.), *Civil Society and the State: New European Perspectives* (London and New York, 1988), pp. 196–7 (my translation).

Such details of the slide into barbarism are frightening. They proved to be not only the prelude to something that had never happened before – the chillingly efficient, well-organized extermination of millions in gas chambers and ovens and labour camps – but also an anticipation of thousands of recorded twentieth-century instances in which the wielders of state violence devoured all remnants of civility, along with their subjects. Future political historians of the twentieth century will hopefully recall what are surely among the most bizarre cases of this potential for extreme violence by (would-be) officials of the modern state: the systematic rape of women by soldiers, often with terrified local men forced at gunpoint to look on; the ritual mutilation of victims, such as cutting off their noses, breasts, ears or penises; and the practice of forcing members of a family group at knife- or gunpoint to kill each other (slowly) in turn, or even forcing parents to maim or kill or hack their children to pieces, and to cook and eat the prepared dish prior to their own execution.[13]

These cases of violence are grotesque reversals of Claude Lévi-Strauss's dictum that primitive cultures are anthropophagic (they 'devour' their adversaries) while modern civilizations are anthropoemic (they segregate, evict, marginalize or 'vomit' their adversaries), but it would be mistaken to conclude that they somehow represent a lapse into 'traditionalism' or 'tribalism'. They are in fact quintessentially modern, not only because of their implication in the struggle for territorially bound state power, but also because they are illustrations of the rational-calculating use of violence as a technique of terrorizing and demoralizing whole populations and preventing them from engaging in organized or premeditated resistance. It is exactly the anthropophagic character of modern forms of violence that has led some observers to draw the pessimistic conclusion that civil societies cannot escape the monopolistic powers of the sovereign state, within whose shadow, as Elias's humbling account implies, each newborn

---

[13] All of these practices are documented in K.B. Wilson, 'Cults of Violence and Counter-Violence in Mozambique', *Journal of Southern African Studies*, vol. 18, no. 3 (September 1992), pp. 527–82.

child is today expected within a few years to do what is virtually impossible: to acquire a sense of non-violent self-control, shame and delicacy which it has taken European populations many centuries to develop.

*   *   *

Zygmunt Bauman's *Modernity and the Holocaust* presents the most sophisticated version of this line of argument. Previous theorists of the modern European civilizing process, Elias included, are charged with ignoring the perversely self-destructive dynamic of violence. The modern civilizing process, typically understood as the slow but steady inculcation of shared norms such as the abhorrence of murder, the disinclination to violent assault, moral responsibility for one's actions in the world and the fear of a guilty conscience, not only results (as Elias concedes) in dangerous concentrations of the means of violence in state hands; it is also a process of insulating the ownership and deployment of violence against moral calculations and, hence, carries within it the seeds of planned cruelty on a mass scale. The civilizing process logically leads to the kind of amoral attitude displayed by Dr Servatius in his summary defence of Adolf Eichmann in Jerusalem: figures like Eichmann are decorated for acts if they triumph over their enemies, whereas they go to the gallows in disgrace if they are defeated.

It follows from this phenomenon of amoral violence, Bauman argues, that zones of civility in everyday life are possible only because somewhere in the wings physical violence is stored up in institutional places and quantities that effectively place it beyond the control of ordinary citizens. Everyday codes of conduct thus mellow mainly because the subjects of state power are constantly threatened with violence in case they are violent – with violence they themselves cannot match or reasonably expect to repulse. The pacification of everyday life renders most people defenceless; they become the playthings of the potentially sinister managers of coercion. In effect, Bauman's thesis is the mirror image of the late-eighteenth-century view of the civilizing process as an upward spiral into civility. Civility and barbarity lie side by side on a down-spiralling continuum of violence. There is, he claims, no dividing line between civilized norms and uncivil abnormality. Civilization should be a synonym for the constant potential, under modern conditions, of political power perfecting itself into the bureaucratic planning and execution of genocide. 'Holocaust-style phenomena must be recognized as legitimate outcomes of [the] civilizing tendency, and its constant potential.'

Bauman is surely right to insist – here he rewords a key thesis in post-Weberian sociological theory in Germany – that totalitarianism is no mere accident on the superhighway of modern progress. His thesis also helpfully points to one of the most disturbing enigmas that the friends of civil society must confront: that there are times and places when civilized manners can and do peacefully cohabit with mass murder. Among the bizarre twentieth-century examples of this enigma (unmentioned by Bauman) is the *Great Gatsby*-style party, held in late April 1935 in Moscow, hosted by the first American Ambassador to the Soviet Union, William C. Bullitt; at this gathering, held at precisely the time that the purges were reaching frenzied proportions, the entire Soviet elite, bar Stalin himself, reportedly socialized with smiling faces, cigarettes and drinks in hand, knowing that the guests included henchmen and victims, many of whom were both. The same bizarre type of occasion, in which civility greets barbarity, is symbolized by the friendly, relaxed atmosphere at Wannsee in January 1942, where Müller, Heydrich, Eichmann and his Nazi colleagues sipped champagne and smoked cigars after a hard day's work deciding the details of how to proceed with the *Endlösung*; and it is typified by the civilized trials of war criminals at Nuremberg, a city that lay in ruins, carpeted by tens of thousands of corpses, whose rotting flesh made local water dangerously undrinkable, as if it were water trickling from a morgue.

*   *   *

These points made by Bauman are salutary. Yet his conclusion that modern civility is the ally of barbarity has its costs, one of which is his dogmatic pessimism. The postulates of 'mutual assistance, solidarity, reciprocal respect etc.', qualities to which Bauman pays lip service (since they are antithetical to totalitarianism) and which are normally considered among the organizing principles of any functioning civil society, are brushed aside conceptually as mere phantoms: in other words, civil society, a category that Bauman needs to rescue modernity from itself, is subjected to a reductionist interpretation that, formally speaking, resembles the Marxian reduction of civil society to bourgeois domination and violence. Not surprisingly, Bauman's conclusions slip into moroseness.

The type of analysis of 'modern civility as barbarity' proffered by Bauman also misses the point that the modern civilizing process contains several potentially productive – if dangerous – contradictions. One of them is the frightening development of techniques of total war and universally devastating means of violence that threaten the very capacity of states and their subjects to secure themselves against the ravages of war. Mechanized total war is an invention of the late eighteenth century that only reached perfection – and the height of self-contradiction – during our long century of violence. Born of all-devouring confrontations at sea, in which the aim is skilfully to destroy one's opponents and their equipment completely, total war unwittingly prompted a brand new possibility. This centred especially on the topic of whether war, or at least certain types of war, is still possible in a world flooded with weaponry, some of which, if used by their respective combatants, would necessarily catapult us from, say, the early-nineteenth-century world of Colonel Shrapnel testing his deadly new fragmenting shell on the wildlife of Foulness Island, into a world in which the use of the latest weapons of war would render (certain forms of) war obsolete, simply because human beings, let alone armies and weapons systems, could no longer continue to exist anywhere on the face of the earth, or at least in certain of its formerly populous regions.

The history of the development of modern weapons systems was from the outset pregnant with this bizarre possibility that violence would beget violence and so threaten the utility of violence. The possibility was finally born with the invention and deployment of nuclear weaponry, the destructive potential of which is symbolized by the dripping flesh, swollen faces and molten and con-fused bodies left behind on the scorched earth of Hiroshima by the swooping Enola Gay one summer's day early in August 1945. Since that day, the principle of annihilation, which recognizes no 'class principle' (Khrushchev), has bedevilled the whole world; the human species has had to contend not only with its own individual mortality but with the possibility of the collective death of humanity. The number of nuclear-tipped states has continued to grow, and there is no end to talk of the benefits and necessary evil of nuclear weaponry, despite a growing body of sober warnings about their dangerously self-contradictory potential.

*   *   *

This self-contradiction within the 'realist' logic governing the interaction of heavily armed nation-states hellbent on permanent rearmament – that it strikes down von Clausewitz's dictum that victory in modern warfare goes to the side that can will itself to survive and persuade its adversary to surrender – is arguably beginning to be recognized worldwide by the men and women of state power. The process is only in its infancy, but it serves as a reminder that the history of modern state building is more complicated than scholars such as Elias and Bauman have supposed, and that the development of an international system of states struggling to monopolize the means of violence within a clearly delimited territory has everywhere been a history of more or less sustained resistance, organized from above and below, to the publicly unaccountable power of potentially violent states. Hobbesian realism should not be allowed to have the last word on the subject of state violence, if only because the mosaic of contradictory tendencies that we loosely call modernity includes striking attempts to invent and deploy non-violent methods of ensuring that the institutions of violence, such as the police and the army, become publicly accountable, and therefore disembodied or 'empty' spaces of power that can be made by citizens to change their ways, precisely because they are in principle neither permanently identified with nor owned by any particular individual or power group, including the government of the day.

The struggle to restrain the means of violence, to subject them to open public controversy and to hinder their unpopular or reckless use, can be understood as a contribution to efforts to minimize the threats of violence confronting civil society from the outside. This attempted democratization of the means of state violence, as it can be called, has multiple historical roots and has relied upon a great variety of overlapping and sometimes conflicting methods of pacification, of which nevertheless two broad subgenres can be identified.

*   *   *

The first takes the form of various political-legal or constitutional experiments with alternatives to the near-dominant Westphalian model of interstate power, according to which whole regions and ultimately the globe itself must perforce be divided territorially among sovereign states enjoying a monopoly of the means of violence, each state being left free to enter into irenic agreements with others, or to make war on those states it declares to be enemies. According to a succession of relatively neglected theorists stretching from Pufendorf and Althusius to Paine, Calhoun, von Seydel and Schmitt, this model of interstate power has either never actually been hegemonic or never deserved to be hegemonic. They are less interested in modern empires, a good comparative history of which has yet to be written, than in the various modern constitutional alternatives – the old Swiss Confederation that lasted from the later medieval period until 1789, the United Provinces of the Netherlands that lasted from 1579 to 1795, the German Bund that lasted from 1815 to 1866 – that have been guided by the broad aim of developing a type of suprastate government founded upon a *foedus* or treaty among states, whose rulers and ruled see the distinct advantages in the practical transcendence of an anarchic system of sovereign states prone constantly to war and threats of war. The Philadelphian model, born of the American colonists' struggle against the British and institutionalized as the United States of America between the establishment of the union (1781–9) and the Civil War (1861–5), is an example that ought to be of interest to contemporary theorists of civil society, since the whole point of this model is to institutionalize the means of violence in such a way that the unaccountable quality of state violence and the bellicose anarchy among states typical of the Westphalian model are overcome.[14] Strong traces of the Philadelphia spirit, especially the will to overcome the violent anarchy of the unregulated nation-state system by means of political-legal regulation and the public apportioning of power over the means of violence, have found their way into such twentieth-century constitutional experiments as the League of Nations, the United Nations and the European Union. They have been supplemented with supranational political-legal arrangements which attempt to criminalize certain forms of state violence. The International Military Tribunals at Nuremberg and Tokyo and, most recently, the Hague International Tribunal, are examples of pathbreaking (if procedurally flawed) efforts to define and to prosecute war crimes, crimes against humanity (such as rape) and genocide.

*   *   *

The twentieth-century assault on the Westphalian model has not only concentrated on reducing the quantity and types of violence within the Hobbesian world of interstate relations. Driven by the maxim that states are increasingly bellicose the more they exercise power violently over their subjects at home, international constitutional efforts have also concentrated on the domestic pacification of states. The Council of Europe, founded in 1949 with three key objectives – pluralist democracy, commitment to the rule of law and the protection of human rights – is something of a model of this strategy, since for the first time anywhere in the world it sought to codify these

[14] See Gerald Stourzh, *Alexander Hamilton and the Idea of Republican Government* (Stanford, 1970); Daniel H. Deudney, 'The Philadelphian System: Sovereignty, Arms Control, and Balance of Power in the American States-Union, circa 1787–1861', *International Organization*, vol. 49, no. 2 (Spring 1995), pp. 191–228; my account of Thomas Paine's advocacy of federalism in the new American republic in *Tom Paine: A Political Life* (New York and London 1995), chapter 7; and my critique of the Philadelphia vision in 'The Philadelphia Model', in Takashi Inoguchi, John Keane and Edward Newman (eds), *The Changing Nature of Democracy* (New York, 1998).

objectives in the European Convention of Human Rights and to provide mechanisms for enforcing them effectively. Observance of these objectives is considered the key condition of a state's membership of the Council of Europe and, unlike most supranational organizations, admission to it is not automatic; applicant states must first accept both its Statute (which embodies the three objectives) and scrutiny of their laws and practices to establish whether in fact the objectives are being fulfilled.

The Council of Europe's role in defending individuals' rights, regardless of their formal citizenship status, goes well beyond scrutinizing individual states' laws and practices at the time of entry. Membership also entails a continuous obligation to observe these rights, which the Council seeks to ensure by means of specific enforcement procedures, including the prospect of a member state, after the exhaustion of domestic remedies, being taken to the quasi-judicial European Commission and the European Court of Human Rights in Strasbourg. Among the unusual aspects of the enforcement process is that violations of human rights, such as freedom from torture, are deemed to extend to potential or actual incidents outside a state's territory (as in cases of deportation or extradition of an individual to a country where he or she is at risk of state violence). The enforcement process also tries to address the fact that, even when a state is deemed to have violated a basic human right, its policing and justice system may carry on as before. It does so through such mechanisms as the Torture Committee, which has the specific mandate of examining, by means of visits, the treatment of individuals deprived of their rights with a view, where necessary, to protecting them from inhuman or degrading treatment or punishment. The Torture Committee works on the assumption that state violence against its subjects flourishes when hidden from the public eye, and its overall strategy is therefore describable as the public exposure or democratization of concealed violence. Although the Committee must give prior notification of a visit to a particular country, that state is obliged to permit its visits unannounced to any place within the state's jurisdiction, including prisons, military barracks, asylum centres, hospitals for the mentally ill and children's homes. The Torture Committee also tries to counter the state's propensity to conceal its violence through the element of surprise, which is reflected in the limited timescales (usually two weeks) of its announced but unscheduled visits. It further relies on the tactics of interviewing allegedly violated individuals in private and alerting local pressure groups to provide additional relevant information. After each visit, the Committee is required to produce a report, whose publication depends upon either the request of the state party – which is becoming the norm – or the unilateral decision of the Committee to embarrass that state by making the report publicly available.

*   *   *

Efforts to restrain the Westphalian model of interstate power and to democratize the means of state violence are not exclusively concentrated within the constitutional sphere. They also arise from within civil society, where they assume the quite different form of public initiatives that aim to problematize and to reduce the quantity and arbitrariness of (threatened) state violence. Whether these initiatives succeed, or to what degree, is not at issue here, for the important point to recognize is that this long century of violence has witnessed, for the first time on any scale, what might be called a civilizing politics: that is, organized citizens' initiatives seeking to ensure that nobody 'owns' or arbitrarily uses the means of state violence against civil societies at home and/or abroad. Those like Elias who ignore this new civilizing politics are usually attached, sometimes without recognizing it, to an image of the modern state first sketched by Hobbes and revived earlier this century in Carl Schmitt's sympathetic interpretation of the modern state as the 'mortal God', as the first artificial product of the modern technological world, as a humanly invented mechanism of command that leads the struggle, if necessary by means of violence, against all domestic and foreign competitor powers, actual or potential.[15] This Hobbesian view of the state is becoming unrealistic. Recent citizens' efforts to

[15] Carl Schmitt, *Der Leviathan in der Staatslehre des Thomas Hobbes*, (Hamburg, 1938).

publicize and denounce the use of rape as a weapon of war, to argue the illegality of nuclear weapons in such bodies as the International Court of Justice or to block the detonation of these weapons by direct action, serve as a reminder that peace is of concern not only to politicians, generals and diplomats, but to citizen-civilians as well.

* * *

These efforts may be seen as part of a broader development during the twentieth century of a civilizing politics that encompasses such diverse themes as campaigns against homicide and the rape of women, violence against children, cruelty to animals and the concealed violence of disciplinary institutions like prisons, asylums and schools. Among the ironic effects of these campaigns is to heighten the shared perception of many citizens that civil society is riddled with dangerous pockets of violence in need of avoidance or containment or treatment or repression or new social policies. In practice, this sense of the omnipresence of violence is reinforced by various factors – from the risk and safety requirements of insurance companies to government 'law and order' campaigns and citizens' willingness to report violence to the authorities – that together have the long-term effect of highlighting to the members of civil society their own propensities to violence. These various factors not only ensure that statistical 'facts' about violence are always and necessarily 'fictitious' (a point appreciated by criminologists); they also cast doubt upon Elias's claim that civilized societies forget their genealogy and take for granted as natural their own civility.

* * *

The point can be toughened: *all known forms of civil society are plagued by endogenous sources of incivility*, so much so that one can propose the empirical-analytic thesis that incivility is a chronic feature of civil societies, one of their typical conditions, and, hence, normatively speaking, a perennial barrier to the actualization of a fully 'civilized' civil society. 'Gradually violence on the part of the existing powers will diminish and obedience to the laws will increase', predicted Kant when reflecting on the advantages of republican government and civil society. 'There will arise in the body politic perhaps more charity and less strife in legal disputes, more reliability in keeping one's word, and so on, partly due to love of honour, partly out of well-understood self-interest.'[16] The presumed or implied positively teleological relationship between civil society and violence in this formulation is unwarranted; civil society, contrary to Kant, is not necessarily synonymous with the drift towards 'perpetual peace'. A highly developed civil society can and normally does contain within itself violent tendencies: that is, patterns of incivility or behaviour prone to violence that can and do threaten to accumulate synergetically to the point where the occasional violence of some against some within a civil society degenerates into the constant violence of all against all of an uncivil society, a state-framed ensemble of social institutions that are not merely prone to be but actually are dominated by uncivil forms of interaction, ranging from everyday rudeness tinged with veiled threats of bodily harm to systematically organized violence. In an uncivil society, civility becomes a scarce resource. There remains a battleground, in which the stronger – thanks to the survival of certain civil liberties – enjoy the licence to twist the arms of the weaker. Under extreme conditions, an uncivil society can even haemorrhage to death. Uncivil war looms.

It should be clear that, when using the old-fashioned adjective 'uncivil', I am not referring to the various forms of action originally described by Henry David Thoreau's *On the Duty of Civil Disobedience* (1849) as civil disobedience: that is, vigorous acts of deliberate law breaking or extroverted acts of disputed legality, whose stated aim is to bring before a public either the alleged illegitimacy or ethical or political indefensibility of certain government laws or corporate or state policies. So understood, civil disobedience is not

---

[16] Immanuel Kant, 'Welchen Ertrag wird der Fortschritt zum besseren dem Menschengeschlecht abwerfen?' (1798), in *Der Streit der Facultäten in drey Abschnitten*, in *Schriften zur Anthropologie, Geschichtsphilosophie, Politik und Pädagogik* (Darmstadt, 1975), part 2, section 2, p. 365.

synonymous with incivility, even though it is often denounced by those who fear or disapprove of it as uncivilized or lawless or violent. Thoreau himself publicly defended a decision not to pay taxes to a government which sanctioned slavery, while Mahatma Gandhi, who did more than anybody in the twentieth century to popularize the strategy of civil disobedience, helped forcibly to obstruct British imperial government; in each case, and in subsequent cases of the use of civil disobedience as a strategy of agitation for change, those who engage in acts of provocation and confrontation are deliberately committed to non-violence as a means of contesting illegitimate power, for the purpose of strengthening civil society.

*   *   *

Within an uncivil society, by contrast, there is certainly no shortage of spaces of interaction for vigorous activities operating at a distance from state institutions. It is precisely that freedom that tends to spawn the growth of violence. But what exactly is the meaning of this much-used, much-abused term 'violence'? Like all concepts in the human sciences, categories like violence can be fatal for the imagination essentially because they provide a potentially false sense of certainty about the world; on the other hand, without such categories, thinking is wounded, sometimes fatally, and it therefore follows that a political theory of violence needs to be aware of the need for sharp-edged categories that are as necessary as they are dangerous. It is essential to recognize that the term 'violence' is notoriously contested, and that its scope and meaning change through time and from space to space: Darnton's gripping account of cat burnings in pre-1789 France and current controversies about cruelty to animals remind us that acts that were once considered in a certain context non-violent and carnavalesque are, at a later moment and in a different context, regarded as strangely cruel curiosities; a similar plasticity of the term violence is displayed in its extension from the core domains of the military and criminal law to other spaces of life and classes of action, as has happened during the past several decades with the remarkable emergence of the term 'domestic violence'.[17] These spatial and temporal variations serve as an unavoidable complication in theorizations of violence. But still I want to insist on the need to preserve its original and essential core meaning, untainted by loose metaphorical allusions (as when a standard or treaty is 'violated' or somebody is said to suffer a 'violent convulsion' or shakes 'violently', or engages in speech acts that are described as 'violent' because they are passionate or immoderate), unhindered by questions of motivation (people can be violent for a bewildering variety of reasons) or legality (violence can be, and is often, not merely the unlawful exercise of physical force), and not weighed down by mistaken, if commonplace, presumptions, such as the conviction that violence against things is somehow equivalent to violence against people, as if people are the same as property.

As used here, the concept of violence has old-fashioned connotations traceable to the earliest (late medieval) English usages of the term (from the Latin *violentia*) to describe 'the exercise of physical force' against someone who is thereby 'interrupted or disturbed' or 'interfered with rudely or roughly' or 'desecrated, dishonoured, profaned, or defiled'. It is important to preserve this older and more precise meaning of violence not only because of its continuing pertinence in a long century of violence, but also because attempts (such as Johan Galtung's) to stretch its meaning to include 'anything avoidable that impedes human self-realization' effectively makes a nonsense of the concept, linking it to a questionable ontological account of 'the satisfaction of human needs' and making it indistinguishable from 'misery', 'alienation' and 'repression'.[18] Violence is better understood as the unwanted physical interference by groups and/or individuals with the bodies of others, which are consequently made to suffer a series of effects ranging from shock, bruises, scratches, swelling or headaches

---

[17] Robert Darnton, *The Great Cat Massacre and Other Episodes in French Cultural History* (Harmondsworth, 1991); Wini Breines and Linda Gordon, 'The New Scholarship on Family Violence', *Signs: Journal of Women in Culture and Society*, vol. 8, no. 3 (Spring 1983), pp. 490–531.

[18] Johan Galtung, *Transarmament and the Cold War: Peace Research and the Peace Movement* (Copenhagen, 1988).

to broken bones, heart attacks, loss of limbs or even death. Violence can, of course, take the form of enforced self-violation (as in suicide or 'voluntary' euthanasia), and it can be consciously intended or half-unintended, the extreme cases of which are injury caused by recklessness or institutionally produced violations of individuals or whole groups. But in each case, violence is a relational act in which the object of violence is treated, involuntarily, not as a subject whose 'otherness' is recognized and respected, but rather as a mere object potentially worthy of bodily harm, or even annihilation. The stipulation that violence is unwanted physical interference with a subject – as when a woman has her thighs forced apart by a man who stuffs her vagina and/or anus with a revoltingly alien organ – is expressed in such sayings as 'He laid violent hands on her' or 'He was in a violent temper'. It is also manifested in cases of institutional violence, such as those analysed by Michel Foucault, in which the bodies of subjects are confined, against their will but in the name of their improvement, in houses of discipline and punishment in which, so to say, violence is redeployed from public sites of punishment, sanitized and camouflaged within the walls of the prison, hospital, asylum.

*   *   *

To emphasize the involuntary character of violence implies that violence is one – extreme – form of the denial of a subject's freedom to act in and upon the world. However that subjectivity and freedom are defined – narrowly liberal or property-centred or European ways of life are not presumed in this discussion – violence obstructs subjects' bodily motion. Violence is thus prima facie incompatible with the civil society rules of complex and differentiated patterns of solidarity, liberty and equality of citizens, since those individual citizens who are violated experience interference with their bodies, which may consequently suffer damage, physically and psychically. While the imagined, historically rooted, collective identities of a civil society (geographic communities or religious groupings, for instance) are damaged or annihilated when their constituent members are violated – violence destroys the mutual interdependence of the living, the dead and the unborn – violence has this effect only because ultimately it bears down on and threatens embodied individuals, who are treated as mere objects, and whose bodies are deemed worthy of a kick and a punch, or a knife, a bullet or a bomb. Those who experience violence against them find in effect that they are treated, as Aristotle put it, as 'a solitary advanced piece in a game of draughts', or (as he says elsewhere) like a wild animal 'meant to be hunted'. Aristotle's formulation, of course, supposed the probability of violence within both the pre-political realm of the *oikos* and the extrapolitical 'barbarian' world beyond the *polis*. 'The world would be a curious place', he remarked, 'if it did not include some elements meant to be free, as well as some that are meant to be subject to control, and if that is its nature any attempt to establish control should be confined to the elements meant for control, and not extended to all.'[19]

Contemporary accounts of civil society arguably need to leave behind this Aristotelian distinction between the (violence-ridden) realm of necessity and the (pacified) realm of freedom. And yet Aristotle's basic insight that violence instrumentalizes potentially speaking and interacting subjects remains compelling. Rephrased in language that he would not have properly understood: a civil society protected and supported by publicly accountable state institutions implies the cultivation of speaking and peacefully interacting subjects, whereas the (at least temporary) effect of violence is to render them mute objects – and often to herd them into death's lair.

The most readily identifiable, 'purest' forms of violence are undoubtedly those acts which result in involuntary death (or what is called in plain speech 'violent death'). Death is the potentially ultimate consequence of violence. For each individual, death is both a terminus and a reference point on the map of life, marking out the intersection of the finite and the infinite. Death may well serve as the point from which individuals evaluate their lives unencumbered by the pressures of

[19] Aristotle, *Politica*, book 1, chapter 2, 1253a; and book 7, chapter 2, 1324b; cf. book 7, chapter 14, 1333a–1334a.

the world; they can reflect upon what they have or have not achieved, what they have become and what might be in store for them. In this sense, death is at the same time birth, for it is precisely in death that life reaches its apogee. There are, of course, lots of different ways of dying. Lucky are those who can die among friends or relatives, with dignity, photographed or filmed with a look of indefinable authority on their brave faces. Unlucky are those – there have been several hundred million during the twentieth century alone – who are robbed of an 'individual death' (Rainer Maria Rilke), whose deaths are forced, anonymous, as if their own deaths die a sudden death, stealing from them the possibility of taking stock of their lives, past, present and future. There are as well lots of different ways of being killed, but only one result: you are dead, you are no more, you are no longer to be found any- where. For someone, somewhere, you may become a statistic; if you are lucky, your photograph and treasured belongings will be held in perpetuity by relatives, friends, colleagues or lovers. But the truth is that those who suffer violent death have been pushed over the edge. Death is their centre of grav ity. It marks the end of their fall. They are no longer on the streets, they are no longer at work, or in their beds or kitchens, or in the arms of their loved ones. They are just blood-stained bodies in back alleys, covered in ants or flies. They are shallow graves dug in fields or bodies dumped into the sea or motion- less hulks on stone slabs. End of story.

* * *

Those who work for a (more) civil society must recognize not only that violence is often the antithesis of civil society, but also that every known form of civil society tends to produce this same violent antithesis, thereby preventing it from becom- ing a haven of non-violent harmony. This inner contradiction within the workings of civil society – that it tends to be a peace- ful haven of incivility – has been obscured by the originally eighteenth-century theory of the upward spiral towards civili- zation and, more recently, by the strange silence about violence within the renaissance of the theory of state and civil society. But what exactly is the source of this troubling contradiction?

The most common explanation resorts to ontological considerations. 'We see even in well-governed states, where there are laws and punishments appointed for offenders,' wrote Hobbes, 'particular men travel not without their sword by their sides for their defences; neither sleep they without shutting not only their doors against fellow subjects, but also their trunks and coffers for fear of domestics.' Incivility is here treated as a primeval energy: 'the condition of Man . . . is a condition of Warre of every one against every one; in which case every one is governed by his own Reason; and there is nothing he can make use of, that may not be a help unto him, in preserving his life against his enemyes; It followeth that in such a condition, every man has a Right to every thing; even to one anothers body.'[20]

Three and a half centuries later, Hobbes's reasoning about human nature still enjoys a reputation. This is partly because we have not yet shed the old bourgeois fascination with neo-Hobbesian themes – Peter Gay's compelling study has shown just how strong was this fascination during the past century[21] – and partly because the view of human nature as violent has a certain intuitive appeal, especially when 'the facts' seem to speak for themselves. What else but dastardly human nature is behind the evil acts perpetrated by government soldiers who chop off their victims' ears or genitals and force them at gunpoint to chew them before suffering execution? Surely the willingness of soldiers to force mothers at gunpoint to shoot their own terrified children through the head before an assembled crowd, only then to shoot the killers and the crowd itself, proves that we have an inborn need to be violent? What else explains the perversely sadistic pleasure of the torturer who places a rat inside his victim, so beginning the slow process of death by cruel humiliation?

*   *   *

[20] Thomas Hobbes, 'Preface to the Reader', *Philosophical Rudiments concerning Government and Society* (London, 1651); and *Leviathan, or The Matter, Forme, and Power of a Common-Wealth Ecclesiastical and Civill* (London, 1651), part 1, chapter 14.

[21] Peter Gay, *The Cultivation of Hatred: The Bourgeois Experience – Victoria to Freud* (London, 1994).

There can be no doubt that in order to understand such acts of violence it is vital to have an understanding of the character structure of the individual perpetrator, who, although he or she usually acts in concert with a wider group of perpetrators, is at some point in the act of violence alone with the victim and driven by inner instincts and thoughts. Armies or gangs alone do not kill, not even when violence is administered by war machines that physically or visually distance the violent from the violated. And yet when seeking to understand why individuals are violent it is equally clear that a distinction needs to be drawn between the two different types of microlevel or 'human nature' explanation, stretching from St Augustine to Freud, that seek to trace the causes of violence to human nature. First, there are those ahistorical ontologies that suppose that Man is essentially wicked (as in Machiavelli's claim that all men at all times are 'ungrateful, changeable, simulators and dissimulators, runaways in danger, eager for gain')[22] and therefore have difficulty side-stepping institutionalist explanations in order to account for why and how individuals and, indeed, whole societies are from time to time pacific, sometimes for extended periods. Second, there are those accounts of human nature that admit that in the here and now human nature is perverted, or even bloodthirsty, but that it could in future, under different institutional circumstances, be diverted or made to assume a quite different, more pacific form, as in William James's proposal that the world would become a safer place if its youth were drafted into mining coal, manning ships, building skyscrapers, washing dishes and laundering clothes.[23]

In either case, the attempt to explain violence with sole reference to human nature is forced to admit the necessity of traditions of explanation of violence that make reference to institutional factors. Broadly speaking, there have been two different types of these explanatory traditions. One of them,

---

[22] Niccolò Machiavelli, *The Prince*, in *Machiavelli: The Chief Works and Others*, trans. Alan Gilbert (Durham, NC, 1965), vol. 1, p. 62.
[23] William James, 'The Moral Equivalent of War', in *Memories and Studies* (New York, 1912), pp. 262–72, 290.

meso-level regime theories, insists that violence on a limited or extended scale derives primarily from the particular, historically specific organizing principles of the state or socioeconomic system: in other words, that violence stems from monarchy (Paine) or despotism (Montesquieu) or capitalism (Marx) or states structured by precapitalist values (Schumpeter) or totalitarian dictatorship (Arendt), and that violence will therefore wither away or at least be attenuated only if and when these particular regime types are replaced by republics or constitutional monarchies or the end of class struggle and the common ownership of the means of production or the renewal of active citizenship. The other type of explanation, *macro-level geopolitical theories*, insists that the ultimate roots of violence are traceable to the permanently decentred international system of states, whose anarchic dynamism reflects the absence of genuinely global regulatory mechanisms and the dominance of a plurality of armed states that periodically draw otherwise civil citizens and states into the vortex of bellicose conflict.

*　*　*

The geopolitical type of explanation, a version of which was championed by Elias, has already been examined above, and I shall therefore move to outline and defend a new version of the meso-level explanation. Even if human nature were either essentially or circumstantially prone to violence, it would be necessary to explain how a particular social formation facilitated or hindered expressions of violence. This problem brings us directly back to the original issue of why civil societies tend to generate from within themselves various types of threatening violence. According to one (originally eighteenth-century) formulation, civil societies are best considered not as caught up in an upward spiral of progress, but rather (as Mirabeau put it) as only a brief apogee in an otherwise tragic 'natural cycle from barbarism to decadence by way of civilization and wealth'.[24] The 'iron law' of cycles of violence first formulated

[24] Honoré-Gabriel Riqueti, Comte de Mirabeau, *L'Ami des hommes ou Traité de la population* (Paris, 1756), p. 176.

by Mirabeau is implausible. It is premodern in inspiration, and is certainly hard to substantiate in either theoretical or empirical terms; the metaphysic of decline and renewal also has obstructive policy implications, since it implies that little or nothing can be done to stem the floods of violence that periodically sweep away the protective walls of civility that maintain peace among citizens. More plausible are those meso-level theories that seek to account for the eruptions of violence by tracing them to the specific institutional structures of civil society. Here another important distinction should be drawn: between *capitalism-centred* explanations and more comprehensive *civil society-centred* explanations.

*   *   *

The most influential example of the former is Marx's emphasis on the conflict potential of the wage-labour/capital relationship. The modern bourgeois era, Marx pointed out, is unique in so far as it effects a separation of the political and social forms of stratification. It subdivides the human species for the first time into social classes; divorces individuals' legal status from their socioeconomic role within civil society (*bürgerliche Gesellschaft*); and sunders each individual into private egoist and public-spirited citizen. By contrast, feudal society had a directly political character. The main elements of civil life (property, the household, forms of labour) assumed the forms of landlordism, estates and corporations. The individual members of feudal society enjoyed no private sphere; their fate was bound up inextricably with the network of interlocking public organizations to which they belonged. The 'throwing off of the political yoke' is a distinguishing mark of modern bourgeois orders. Civil society, the realm of private needs and interests, waged labour and private right, is emancipated from political control, and becomes the basis and presupposition of the modern state.

Civil society is represented by Marx – correctly – as a contingent historical phenomenon, and not as a naturally given state of affairs. Modern, state-guaranteed civil societies do not conform to eternal laws of nature, and they certainly do not arise from their members' propensity for society. They are historically determinate entities, characterized by particular forms and relations of production, class divisions and struggles, and protected for a time by corresponding political-legal mechanisms. Not only are bourgeois civil societies products of modern times. Their life expectancy is limited inasmuch as they give birth to the proletariat, the class with radical chains, the class in civil society that is not of civil society, the potentially universal class that signals the dissolution of all classes, if need be through violence. Although he was not alone in this conviction, Marx was right to pinpoint the wage-labour/capital relationship as a potential point of violent antagonism within modern civil societies. The Marxian theses on civil society are nevertheless riddled with problems – outlined above – among which are Marx's mistaken assumptions that lumpenproletarian and proletarian mugging and murder would give way to the organized militancy of the working class, and his poor grasp of both the violence-producing and shock-absorbing potential of non-market institutions within civil society.

In well-established civil societies, certainly, there is comparatively limited scope for the display of strong feelings or strong antipathies towards people, let alone heated anger, wild hatred or the urge to belt someone over the head. Wherever stress-induced tensions develop, they tend to be absorbed or sublimated into the social structures, and civility prevails, or so Elias argues:

> Most human societies, as far as one can see, develop some coun-
> ter-measures against stress-tensions they themselves generate.
> In the case of societies at a relatively late level of civilization,
> that is with relatively stable, even and temperate restraints all
> round and with strong sublimatory demands, one can usually
> observe a considerable variety of leisure activities with that
> function, of which sport is one.[25]

If that is so, then the fundamental question remains un-
answered: Why do the shock-absorbing institutions of civil

[25] Norbert Elias, 'Introduction', in Norbert Elias and Eric Dunning, *Quest for Excitement: Sport and Leisure in the Civilizing Process* (Oxford and Cambridge, Mass., 1993), p. 41.

societies tend to be overburdened, such that they generate from within their own structures patterns of violence that contradict the freedom, solidarity and civility which otherwise make them so attractive?

*   *   *

The openness that is characteristic of all civil societies – their nurturing of a plurality of forms of life that are themselves experienced as contingent – is arguably at the root of their tendency to violence. The well-recognized fact that they enable groups to organize for the pursuit of wealth and power, for instance, has made their capitalist economies not only restlessly dynamic at home, but also prone to expansion on a global scale, one consequence of which has been the widespread exporting of violence to tribes, regions, nations and whole civilizations considered rude or savage. Modern civil societies have provided handsome opportunities for certain power groups tempted by dreams of expansionism, and this has ensured that the whole modern history of colonization and bullying of the uncivilized has been riddled with violence, to the point where it may be said, with a touch of bitter irony, that the current worldwide appeal of civil society is the bastard child of the violence of metropolitan civility.

The legal or informal freedom to associate in complex ways that is afforded the members of any civil society also makes them prone to violence at home. There are several reasons for this. One of them has to do with the fact that civil societies, ideal-typically conceived, are complex and dynamic webs of social institutions in which the opacity of the social ensemble – citizens' inability to conceive, let alone grasp, the totality of social life – combined with the chronic uncertainty of key aspects of life (employment and investment patterns, who will govern after the next elections, the contingent identity of one's self and one's household) makes their members prone to stress, anxiety and revenge. All modern civil societies are more or less caught in the grip of what Heinrich von Kleist called the 'fragile constitution of the world' (*die gebrechliche Einrichtung der Welt*), and such fragility increases the probability that the customary moral sanctions and restraints upon the resort to violence can be rejected or avoided by some of their members. Especially when combined with social discrimination, say in the form of racial prejudice and joblessness, this amoral anxiety and frustration encourages violent responses, sometimes directed by the disadvantaged against themselves. This is probably one reason why the homicide rate for black Americans is seven times higher than for whites, why nearly two-thirds of persons arrested for murder and violent robbery are black and why half the population of US gaols is black, even though blacks represent only 12 per cent of the overall population. The effect of such patterns is to create archipelagos of incivility within an otherwise civil society that contains certain medieval features. Just as in the Middle Ages many men always carried arms, never lightly ventured beyond the towns and feared that the forests were full of frightening foes, so the white middle-class inhabitants of cities such as New York – where there are some 2,000 murders each year, a figure nearly as high as the total number of killings in the whole of Northern Ireland since the end of the 1960s – never get off the subway in Harlem by mistake, never go to the South Bronx, never take the subway alone after midnight (or earlier, if they are women) and never set foot in Central Park after dark.

*   *   *

The increasing availability and cheapness of means of violence within existing civil societies no doubt fuels this tendency, although the degree to which it does so remains uncertain, which is why hysterical claims about the need for gun control should be tempered with reflection on both the multiple roots and forms of violence and the ways in which the resort to arms is symptomatic of the deeper tendency of civil societies to unnerve and disorientate their members. Among the least obvious ways in which the fragile openness of civil societies contributes to their apparently violent character is the way in which their sophisticated means of public and private communication ensure that images of violence are circulated more or less freely to large numbers of people. That is to say, freedom of communication within civil society ensures that violence against others can and is often turned into entertainment: that is, made the object of popular fascination, thrill and pleasure. The anomic violence that is regularly produced within civil societies is not always, and sometimes rarely, experienced as loss or a lapse into nothingness. The hard fact is that violence can be experienced as pleasure, as fulfilment, as a form of excitement that tickles the fancy of not only the violated – expressed in masochistic pleasure – but also the violent and the witnesses of acts of violence. Individuals who are violent, alone with their victims, sometimes treat their actions as entertainment, as in the case (described by Arthur Miller) of the misfit

> stuck with his boredom, stuck inside it, stuck to it, until for two or three minutes he 'lives'; he goes on a raid around the corner and feels the thrill of risking his skin or his life as he smashes a bottle filled with gasoline on some other kid's head. It is life . . . standing around with nothing coming up is as close to dying as you can get.[26]

Group pleasure in being violent – exemplified by sljivovica-swilling Serbian soldiers singing their way through scores of daily murders – is frequently reported. So too is the pleasure of those witnessing the spectacle of violence.

Contrary to the claims of contemporary campaigners against violence in the media, the packaging and marketing of violence as entertainment is an old phenomenon traceable to the middle of the eighteenth century. Pay-TV sexual murders, Mortal Kombat video games, vomit-provoking splatter films and musicians who cavort with death, safety pins jammed through their bloodied noses, singing of destruction, midnight ramblers and psychokillers, are ancient themes of modern popular culture. The tradition of entertaining violence stretches back through films such as *Night of the Living Dead* and *Psycho* to magazine ghost stories, horrid melodramas, newspaper sensationalism and the Gothic literature and Graveyard poets of the period of Enlightenment. There is admittedly little

[26] Arthur Miller, *The Misfits* (London, 1961), p. 51.

research on the history of these public representations of violence, but it is clear that in modern times scandals generated by violence are older than the trials of O.J. Simpson and the Yorkshire Ripper. The scaffold, for example, was a dominant emotive symbol in early nineteenth-century England. The totemic image of the 'hanged man' pervaded popular culture, appearing on tarot cards, in dream books and in Punch and Judy shows; the tanned skin of the executed was used to bind books about his or her crime; and death masks of hanged criminals attracted big crowds at Madame Tussaud's. A parallel transformation of violence into entertainment, this time involving the violated female corpse, was evident in Weimar Germany, whose civil society, consumed by fear of inside and outside threats, was riveted by Jack the Ripper's deeds in Wedekind's Lulu plays, Otto Dix's paintings of disembowelled prostitutes and Alfred Döblin's sexualization of the murder of Rosa Luxemburg.[27]

With the advent of mass circulation and niche-marketed electronic media operating on a global scale, the age span, size and spatial reach of audiences potentially interested in violent entertainment arguably grows exponentially, to the point where the spectators of violence virtually anywhere in the world can be titillated by hair-raising gore so explicit that it seems unsurpassable in terms of technical perfection and verisimilitude. Why so many millions – gasping and shuddering involuntarily, cold sweat on their brows, upstanding hairs on the nape of their necks – are fascinated by the violent things they might otherwise be expected to run screaming from is an enigma that prima facie lends credence to the originally Freudian thesis of the uncanny (*das Unheimlich*). According

[27] See the account, which is based upon source materials from newspapers, criminal archives and popular ballads, by Gatrell, *The Hanging Tree*, op. cit. The nineteenth-century development of unbridled newspaper sensationalism of acts of violence – the insistence on the hot currency of the news, claims for the unique ferocity of murders, the reportage of gruesome details – is traced in Thomas Boyle, *Black Swine in the Sewers of Hampstead: Beneath the Surface of Victorian Sensationalism* (New York, 1989). The Weimar fetish of violence against women is documented in Maria Tatar, *Lustmord: Sexual Murder in Weimar Germany* (Princeton, NJ, 1995).

to this thesis, death, for which there is no known cure and which is the inevitable destiny of all individuals, may well be 'kept from sight . . . withheld from others', but that very rendering of death as a stranger boomerangs on the individual, heightening his or her sense that death, the ultimate consequence of violence, is 'uncomfortable, uneasy, gloomy, dismal . . . ghastly'.[28] Freud supposed, misleadingly, that the experience of the uncanny, the primitive fear of the dead that inhabits the strange realm between the living and the dead, was a universal human experience. He did not see that the uncanny in fact assumes different historical forms, and that in premodern systems definitions of the uncanny tend to be monopolized and strictly defined by core institutions such as religious authorities, warrior classes and local communities. Understood in this more historically sensitive way, the theory of the uncanny has a striking implication for theories of the modern civilizing process, which need to be reformulated thus: the invention and growth of modern forms of civil society cannot be described as a process synonymous with the growing invisibility and extrusion of violence into the state sphere. Precisely because the power to define the uncanny is no longer monopolized by well-defined authorities – the uncanny becomes homeless – there develops a dialectic of civility in which the visible reduction and practical removal of various forms of violence from civil society coincides with the heightened media visibility and sensuous appreciation of simulated or virtual violence by the citizens of that society, who get qualitatively less solace from worn-out platitudes about salvation and the afterlife.

* * *

What, if anything, can be done about the problem of incivility? Can we envisage a world where there is more civility than at present? Can uncivil war or even violence itself ever be eliminated from human affairs? Can civil societies be made

---

[28] Sigmund Freud, 'The Uncanny' (1919), in *The Standard Edition of the Complete Psychological Works*, ed. James Strachey (London, 1955), vol. XVII, pp. 219–52.

more civil? These are big and hard questions, for which there are no easy answers. It is certainly not the job of political reflection to legislate detailed policy proposals or to advance political strategies and tactics, but it can usefully clarify and highlight the probable advantages and disadvantages of responding to these vital questions in certain ways.

In the dirty business of violence, perspectives on civil society should especially concentrate on defining what should *not* be done and sketching the corresponding ways of thinking and acting that ensure that such mistakes are avoided. So, for example, the prepolitical temptation to resort to pessimistic ontologies ('Individuals are naturally evil', 'We are all creatures of original sin', and so on) or to utopian wishes ('Peace can come, for all men and women are basically good') should be resisted. Although the latter keep alive the important principle of reducing the quantity and intensity of violence in a world riddled with violence, they are bound to disappoint. They are as impractical as the imaginings of a John Lennon song cut into the tearful ending of a feature film about the killing fields of uncivil Cambodia – or as utopian as the worn-out vision, stretching from Plato's *Republic* to Rousseau's *Considérations sur le gouvernement de Pologne*, of a small political community of patriotic and potentially armed citizens, who live in isolation from other political communities, who have no external military or commercial ambitions, and whose concern for non-violent perfection is matched by a certain superiority complex and mistrust of foreigners, which binds them together into a freedom-loving citizenry of potential warriors emancipated from the curse of war.

* * *

The uncivil tendencies of actually existing civil societies are indeed grist to the mill of pessimistic ontologies, which, however, suffer from their indiscriminate acceptance of 'the facts' to prove their fancy, a lack of interest in the motivations of those who kill and are killed, and ignorance of the historical foundations of their presumption. At their best, pessimistic ontologies are no better than holding operations, or alibis, and that is why they meld easily into private antidotes to incivility. Their function, whether intended or not, is often to disarm consciences, to persuade others that really nothing can be done, except for the strategy of putting trust in law and order or opting for a private solution (purchasing a corrugated iron garage in Moscow, employing security staff in London or Tokyo or Abidjan, paying protection money to a warlord in Rio de Janeiro), hoping for the best, which in practice means offloading violence on to others.

There are signs, in some regions and many local communities, that pessimistic ontologies are in fact the ideological accomplices of a long-term trend towards the scattering of violence, whereby the day-to-day defence of society against imaginary or actual threats of violence is passing into the hands of a booming security business, to the point where it is even possible to imagine times and places where quite a few states' monopoly of the means of violence will be permanently eroded by, or fundamentally supplemented with, new forms of *condottieri*. Admittedly this thought should be handled with care, since the long and bloody struggle of modern state builders to monopolize the means of violence within a given territory has constantly been resisted by urban militias, private armies, armed mercantile companies, privateers, fiscal agents and armies of regional lords and rival claimants to royal power.[29] There are nevertheless plenty of documented cases in which the contemporary structures of state power, government policy making and civil society are becoming twisted and deformed into grotesque shapes by gun-wielding gangs and cartels.

Within both civil and uncivil societies, the possible forms of *condottieri* are highly variable, ranging from uniformed private enterprise security agents wielding walkie-talkies and (where permitted) with guns on their hips, to armed gangs, such as those under the tutelage of rough trade warlords. In every case, however, these private solutions to the dangers of incivility are self-contradictory, since they bring violence, or threatened violence, into the heart of social life. As antidotes to violence, private solutions are also unjust: they serve to

---

[29] Janice E. Thomson, *Mercenaries, Pirates, and Sovereigns: State-Building and Extraterritorial Violence in Early Modern Europe* (Princeton, NJ, 1994).

offload threatened or actual violence on to others, who are supposed to cope as best they can, if they can. Private solutions always remain private. They relegate some to the probability of cruel encounters and bloody deaths; the lucky others are free to live in luxury in laagers, behind compound walls, surrounded by armed security guards, Balaclavaed soldiers, sniffer dogs, electronic alarms and barbed wire, with loaded guns under the bed.

*　*　*

So the fundamental question remains: Can anything be done to prevent or to reduce incivility, particularly when it threatens whole populations? There are many possible methods of dealing effectively with incivility in both its milder and murderous forms. Legislator-like theoretical reflection on these methods is again unwise since, as has already been emphasized, they will necessarily vary according to time and place and the particular form of violence in question. For instance, certain uncivil wars – of the kind that unfolded in recent years in the Lebanon, Afghanistan, Rwanda and Bosnia-Herzegovina – may in future be stoppable through outside military intervention, whereas others may be best ended, with a minimum of violence and a maximum of justice, by the withdrawal of outside forces.[30] In certain contexts – Bosnia-Herzegovina, for instance – the practical construction of something like a sovereign territorial state is a fundamental condition of the cessation of uncivil war and the re-creation of the molecular structures of a civil society; in other contexts – for instance, the trumped-up battle of Britain against Argentina in the Malvinas war – attempts to shore up the fiction of a sovereign territorial state have bizarre consequences that end in pointless bloodshed. By contrast, in milder cases of incivility, such as common assaults, those who have committed an act of violence can be arrested by the police, questioned, released with a caution or dealt with through the law courts and perhaps imprisoned; and so on.

In the face of such complexity, the political goal of crafting

---

[30] See my *Reflections on Violence*, op. cit., pp. 131–85.

civil societies by reducing and eliminating violence will be effective only to the extent that it tries to cultivate a plurality of strategies, ranging from macrolevel agreements concerning arms reduction, war crimes tribunals and the need for regional integration of previously sovereign states, to microlevel laws against bodily harassment and everyday violence – for instance, against women, ethnic groups, children, gays and lesbians. In every case, or so I want to argue, these tactics will remain inadequately developed or less than effective – or more likely drift into authoritarian 'law and order' strategies – unless cultures of civility are cultivated at the level of civil society. The danger of authoritarianism should not be underestimated, for especially in the old democracies there are presently signs of a strengthening consensus that criminal violence is a growing pathology, and that its obscure causes place it beyond realistic hope of remedy. 'The very high crime rate of young black males is an aspect of the pathological situation of the black underclass, but there do not appear to be any remedies for this situation that are at once politically feasible and likely to work', writes a well-known Chief Judge in the US Court of Appeals, adding that 'there is no feasible method of preventing parents from beating their children, and also it is unclear whether the beating causes the later violence or the beating and the violence are consequences of the genetic endowment shared by the parents and their children'. These premises lead easily to the conclusion that violence should greet violence. 'Decades of unsuccessful experimentation with different types of rehabilitative programmes have demonstrated the practical futility of the rehabilitative approach and, in the process, have largely discredited criminology as a discipline.' It is said that multivariate data analyses conducted by social scientists prove that 'punishment reduces crime both through deterrence and through incapacitation', and it follows that getting tougher is the right course of action. Juries should be invited to infer from criminal defendants' refusals to testify that they have something to hide. Evidence obtained by the authorities in violation of the law should be considered reliable. Consideration should be given to extending the death penalty to crimes other than unusually brutal or wanton murders. And the costly protraction of criminal proceedings, especially in death cases, where (in the United States) intervals of ten years between sentence and execution are common and intervals of twenty years are not uncommon, must be stopped.[31]

*   *   *

The premise and conclusion of this type of reasoning are questionable, and certainly if its authoritarian or 'get violent with violence' potential is to be contained, the task of fostering widespread recognition of the various kinds of negative effects of incivility and the wide-ranging and more or less effective remedies for incivility is arguably a key priority. I want to emphasize that the cultivation of *public spheres of controversy*, in which the violent exercise of power over others is resisted initially by civilian-citizens' efforts to monitor it non-violently, is a basic condition for reducing or eliminating incivility. Certainly, the tactic of publicizing violence can help minimize the chances of its return, in no small measure because of the quadruple propensity of public spheres. The public spheres of civil society can help to cultivate shared memories of times past when terrible things were done to people. They can heighten citizens' and governments' awareness of the nature and extent of actually existing incivilities. The public spheres of civil society can certainly canvass and circulate to other citizens ethical judgements about whether or not (or under what conditions) a certain form of violence – by the police, for instance – is justified. And public spheres can encourage the formulation of shrewd remedies for incivility, particularly those that are mindful of the complexity of the whole subject, but are still determined to *civilize* civil societies because they know that violence is no friend of democratic institutions.

---

[31] Richard Posner, 'The Most Punitive Nation: A Few Modest Proposals for Lowering the US Crime Rate', *Times Literary Supplement*, no. 4822 (1 September 1995), pp. 3–4.

Publicity

To link violence and public spheres of controversy is to rediscover a theme of early modern political thought that is in turn traceable to the Roman legal system, with its emphasis on the inviolability of peacefully negotiated agreements and treaties (*pacta sunt servanda*), and ultimately to the Greek conviction that public life and violence had nothing in common, essentially because men distinguish themselves from the animals by virtue of their capacity for speech (*lexis*) and action (*praxis*) and, thus, by their propensity for publicly banding together into a *polis* of citizens protected from physical violence by walls around their city. This critical insight – that violence and public speech and action are opposites – is nowadays kept alive, and implicitly acknowledged by the lip service that is often paid to the point that a public sphere backed by a free communications system is vital to the life of a civil society.[1]

Unfortunately, few detailed analyses of the relationship between civil society and 'the public sphere' exist. This is especially regrettable – and urgently needs to be remedied – because we are living in times in which spatial frameworks of commu-

[1] A characteristic example is the (otherwise convincing) definition of civil society as 'social institutions such as markets and voluntary associations and a public sphere which are outside the direct control, in a full or in a mitigated sense, of the state', in Víctor M. Pérez-Díaz, *The Return of Civil Society: The Emergence of Democratic Spain*, op. cit., p. 57. See also Craig Calhoun, 'Civil Society and the Public Sphere', *Public Culture*, no. 5 (1993), pp. 267–80.

nication are in a state of upheaval. The old hegemony of state-structured and territorially-bound public life mediated by radio, television, newspapers and books is rapidly being eroded. In its place are developing a multiplicity of networked spaces of communication which render obsolete the conventional ideal of a unified public sphere and its corresponding vision of a republic of citizens striving to live up to some 'public good'. This restructuring of communicative space arguably forces us to revise our understanding of public life and its 'partner' terms, such as public opinion, public life and the public good. It is especially imperative to recall their genealogy, for an understanding of the history of these terms deepens our appreciation of their multiple meanings, empirical utility and normative potential – and the political pitfalls of using early modern terms such as 'the public sphere' in the much-changed circumstances of the late twentieth century.

*   *   *

Broadly speaking, in modern times there have been three overlapping phases in the invention, refinement and popularization of the concept of the public sphere and its 'partner' terms. Phase one coincides with the early modern struggle against despotic states in the European region. The language of 'the public', 'public virtue' and 'public opinion' was a weapon in support of 'liberty of the press' and other publicly shared freedoms. Talk of 'the public' was directed against monarchs and courts suspected of acting arbitrarily, abusing their power and furthering their 'private,' selfish interests at the expense of the realm. During the seventeeth and eighteenth centuries, the normative ideal of the public sphere – a realm of life in which citizens invented their identities under the shadow of state power – was a central theme of the republican politics of the middling classes. Republicans like the 'Commonwealthmen' simultaneously looked back to the Roman republic (and sometimes to the Greek *polis*) and forward to a world without mean-spirited executive power, standing armies and clericalism.[2] Republicans were sharply criti-

---

[2] Caroline Robbins, *The Eighteenth-Century Commonwealthmen: Studies in the Transmission, Deployment and Circumstance of English Liberal Thought*

cal of the ways in which absolutism induced apathy among its subjects, promoted conformity in matters of religion and state-craft, and corrupted its rulers, to the point (as Molesworth emphasized in his attack on Danish absolutism) where even the town clocks of Copenhagen chimed in unison with the time-pieces of the palace. Republicans accordingly emphasized the importance of cultivating public virtue and public spirit. Con-forming to the remark of the Marquis de Condorcet that 'if kings and priests had realized the potential of printing to un-mask and dethrone them, they would have stifled it at birth', republicans worked for the radical reform of existing polities by means of the right of free expression of citizens and consti-tutional devices to secure the rule of law, mixed government and freedom from 'party' and 'faction' – especially that pro-moting internal dissension and the 'private' designs of mon-archs, ministers and ambitious men of wealth.

*   *   *

Phase two: With the growing power and dynamism of modern capitalist economies, the ideal of the public sphere came to be used principally to criticize the monopoly grip of commodity production and consumption upon areas of civil life thought to be in need of protection from considerations of rationally cal-culated profit and loss. My *Public Life and Late Capitalism* (1984) traced the growing concern within twentieth-century German political thought, especially after the death of Max Weber, to define and to protect a public sphere against the expanding power of organized capitalism, advertising agencies and other professional bodies bent on divining 'public opinion' and mak-ing it speak in their favour. There are numerous examples of this concern with the public sphere. Ferdinand Tonnies's *Kritik der öffentlichen Meinung* (1922) highlighted the dangers of dei-fying public opinion in an era in which organized interests, es-pecially the capitalist press, profited from its manipulation. Karl Jaspers' *Philosophy is for Everyman* (1960) defended the value

---

from the Restoration of Charles II until the War with the Thirteen Colonies (Cambridge, Mass., 1959).

of 'unlimited communication' in an age of market-driven, rational calculation. Hannah Arendt's *Vita Activa* (1960) mourned the modern loss of public life, understood as the capacity of citizens to speak and to interact for the purpose of defining and redefining how they wish to live together in common; according to Arendt, such public interaction has been gradually corroded in modern times by the acid of consumerism trickling through a society of labourers ignorant of the joys and freedoms that result from communicating in public about matters of public importance. Jürgen Habermas's *Strukturwandel der Öffentlichkeit* refined and extended this pessimistic thesis by tracing the rise in early modern Europe of a bourgeois public sphere and the subsequent 'replacement of a reading public that debated critically about matters of culture by the mass public of culture consumers'.[3] Common to each of these interpretations of public life is the insistence that civil societies dominated by commodity-structured economies encourage moral selfishness and disregard of the public good; maximize the time citizens are compulsorily bound to paid labour, thereby making it difficult for them to be involved as citizens in public life; and promote ignorance and deception through profit-driven media manipulation.

*   *   *

Phase three: The first two phases of defining and defending the public sphere highlighted, respectively, the uniquely modern problems of territorially defined state power unaccountable to its citizens and the business-biased egoism of a civil society dominated by organized market capitalism. During the third, most recent phase of usage of the public sphere concept, these twin problems characteristic of modern societies are simultaneously emphasized and the public sphere ideal is linked to the institution of public service broadcasting, which is seen to have an elective affinity with public life and to be the best guarantee of its survival in the era of state-organized, consumer capitalism.

[3] Jürgen Habermas, *Strukturwandel der Öffentlichkeit: Untersuchungen zu einer Kategorie der bürgerlichen Gesellschaft* (Neuwied, 1962), p. 168.

The 'Westminster School' of Nicholas Garnham, Paddy Scannell and other researchers has arguably done most to invent, refine and popularize this third version of the theory of the public sphere. Among its most influential contributions is a series of pathbreaking essays by Nicholas Garnham, who proposes the thesis that debate about broadcasting policy has hitherto been conducted too narrowly in terms of the state/market dualism. Borrowing explicitly from Habermas (who curiously ignored the public service broadcasting model), Garnham argues for a third term, 'the public sphere', for the analytic-empirical and normative purpose of identifying a 'space for a rational and universalistic politics distinct from both the economy and the state'. Garnham insists that the best guarantor of such a politics is the public service broadcasting model, which is designed to mediate and counterbalance state and corporate power, and can in fact do so because it is bound by the imperative of neither maximization of political power nor maximization of profit. While Garnham admits that the actual practice of public service broadcasting is an imperfect realization of the Habermasian ideal of a public sphere of deliberating citizens, he is adamant about its superiority

> to the market as a means of providing all citizens, whatever their wealth or geographical location, equal access to a wide range of high-quality entertainment, information and education, and as a means of ensuring that the aim of the programme producer is the satisfaction of a range of audience tastes rather than only those tastes that show the largest profit.[4]

Market-driven media, Garnham insists, are inimical to public life. In stark contrast to public service broadcasting, market-driven media narrow the scope of what it is possible to say publicly. The number of enterprises which control (or strongly influence) the production and circulation of information and culture is reduced; inequitable power relationships develop

---

[4] Nicholas Garnham, *Capitalism and Communication: Global Culture and the Economics of Information* (London, 1990), p. 120.

between dominant, metropolitan enterprises and cultures and subordinate and peripheral identities; and these market-produced inequalities in turn reinforce deep-rooted social inequalities, which future market-driven technological change in the field of communications will almost certainly deepen – unless the castles of public service broadcasting are protected through guaranteed tax-based funding.

*   *   *

The proposed defence of the public sphere through public service media accurately spots the limits of market rhetoric and practice.[5] It is, moreover, an important contribution to the task of clarifying and amplifying publicly felt concerns about the future of electronic media in the old democracies of such countries as Italy, Britain, France and the Netherlands. The proposed defence of public life also serves as a vital reminder of the important practical achievements of public service media. The twentieth-century project of providing a service of mixed programmes on national radio and television channels, available to all citizens, often in the face of severe technical problems and pressing financial constraints – as Garnham and many others have argued – has kept alive public spirit and widened the horizons of citizens' awareness of the world. For half a century, the 'provision of basic services' (*Grundversorgung*, as the German Federal Constitutional Court put it) helped to decommodify electronic media. It reduced the role of budget-conscious accounting and corporate greed as the principal qualities necessary to media management. The public service model also enforced specific national rules covering such matters as the amount and type of advertising, political access, 'balanced' news coverage and quotas of foreign programming. It succeeded for a time in protecting employment levels in the national broadcasting industries of countries such as the Netherlands, Canada, Norway, Britain and the Federal Republic of Germany. The public service model – partly in response to challenges posed by market-based

[5] Compare my *The Media and Democracy* (Cambridge and Cambridge, Mass., 1991), pp. 52–91.

tabloid media – also legitimized the presence of ordinary citizens in programmes dealing with controversial issues. It helped to make respectable the vernacular styles of civil society by publicizing the pleasures of ordinariness and creating entertainment out of civilians playing games, talking about their private experiences, or immersing themselves in events as disparate as tennis matches, skiing competitions, religious ceremonies, and dancing to rap, rock and reggae.

While these achievements of the public service model are impressive, there are major problems inherent in the argument that existing public service media are a bulwark of the public sphere. For reasons of space, I shall set aside questions about the fault lines evident in Garnham's attempt to synthesize an originally seventeenth- and eighteenth-century ideal with the peculiarly twentieth-century practice of electronic broadcasting.[6] I also want deliberately to overlook other bundles of problems, internal to Garnham's account, such as his silence about the rise and survival of public controversy within the market-dominated sector of print and broadcasting media, or the question of whether a 'rational' and universalistic politics' was descriptive of either the intended aim or the actual practice of public service broadcasting in its heyday. I shall instead concentrate for a moment on the mounting difficulties faced by contemporary public service broadcasting and, hence, on the perilous strategy of attempting to tie the fortunes of the public sphere ideal to an ailing institution.

*   *   *

There is today a long-term crisis settling on the public service model. The status quo is ceasing to be an option. Public service media in Europe and elsewhere are slipping and sliding into a profound identity crisis – the same identity crisis that from the beginning has dogged American public service media, which have suffered permanent insecurities about their financial basis, legal status and public role. Deeply uncertain about their sources of funding and the scope and nature of

---

[6] See my critical review of the work of Michael Sandel in the *Times Higher Education Supplement* (London), 4 October 1996, p. 26.

their contemporary political role, European public service media are enmeshed in a wider political problem, evident in all the old democracies, in which political parties, professional associations, trade unions, churches and other means of defining, projecting and re-presenting citizens' opinions to decision makers are either losing their vibrance or prompting new disputes about their own degree of 'representativeness'. Such controversies about the best means of publicly re-presenting citizens' opinions are symptomatic of an upswing in the modern democratic revolution first outlined by Tocqueville; contrary to many western observers, the defeat of the Soviet Empire, the chief enemy of parliamentary democracy, is leading not to spontaneous outbursts of self-satisfied applause within the old democracies, but to loud questioning of the legitimacy and effectiveness of the entrenched procedures of liberal democracy.

*   *   *

The contemporary malaise of public service broadcasting has several deep-seated causes, three of which bear directly on the theory of civil society and the public sphere:

(1)   Fiscal squeeze: The financial footings of public service broadcasting in the European region are tending to crack and crumble. As Nowak, Blumler and others have shown, licence fee income increases, which resulted during much of the postwar period from the steady diffusion throughout civil society of black-and-white and then colour sets, peaked during the 1970s.[7] With the saturation of households with televisions and radios, the onset of inflation, the proportionately steeper increases in programme production costs, and government cutbacks, licence fee revenue then began to decline in real terms – for example, by 30 per cent during the period from 1972–3 until 1983–4 in Sweden. This fiscal squeeze not only pinched the prospects for a vigorous public service response to those

---

[7] See for example, K. Nowak, 'Television in Sweden: Position and Prospects', in Jay Blumler and T.J. Nossiter (eds), *Broadcasting Finance in Transition: A Comparative Handbook* (New York, 1991), pp. 235–59.

critics favouring 'deregulation', for whom market competition and more advertising are the key conditions of press and broadcasting freedom, understood as private broadcasters' freedom from state interference. The long-term fiscal squeeze also ruled out any sustained involvement of public service broadcasters in the current technological revolution – except here and there, as exemplified by modest teletext initiatives or satellite services operated by the BBC and the German broadcasters, ARD and ZDF. Most of the pioneering interventions in the field of communications were consequently left in the hands of national and international private entrepreneurs – an instructive symbol of which was the inability of BSB, the British satellite operation licensed as a public service venture by the Independent Broadcasting Authority, to survive cut-throat financial competition from Rupert Murdoch's Sky television. Finally, the long-term fiscal squeeze on public service broadcasters has forced them to intensify co-production deals, to privatize or subcontract parts of their programming and production facilities, to engage in international marketing ventures, and in general to speak the language of profit-conscious business executives. Such trends toward 'self-commercialization' arguably weaken the legitimacy of the public service model by diluting its programming distinctiveness and heartening deregulators in their crusade to marginalize public media.

(2)   Legitimacy problems: Public service broadcasters could in principle exercise the option of publicly campaigning to renew the appeal of their activities, but in practice such fightbacks tend to be hamstrung by a growing legitimacy problem. Defenders of the existing public service model typically understate the ways in which the alleged 'balance', 'quality' standards and universalism of existing public service media are routinely perceived by certain audiences as 'unrepresentative'. For their part, public service broadcasters routinely perceive that the repertoire of programmes channelled through existing public service media cannot satisfy the multitude of opinions in a complex (if less than fully pluralist) civil society in motion. In other words, both audiences and broadcasters

sense that the public service claim to representativeness is in fact a defence of *virtual representation* of a fictive whole, a resort to programming which simulates the actual opinions and tastes of *some* of those at whom it is directed. The fate of music programming on public service radio well illustrates this legitimation problem. Although, for obvious reasons, music has always occupied the bulk of radio time, it has proved impossible in the long run to provide programming with general appeal on public service radio because in any one country a nationally shared musical culture has never existed in the past, and certainly does not exist in the present. Different forms of music appeal to different publics, whose dislikes are often as strong as their likes, and that is why the twentieth-century history of public service radio has been the history of the gradual recognition of the fragmentation of mass audiences into different taste publics of civil society. Trends in the world of music illustrate the key point here: the public service model corsets its audiences and regularly violates its own principle of equality of access for all to entertainment, current affairs and cultural programming in a common public domain. The corset is tightened further by the fact that, for reasons of government pressures, threatened litigation and a stated commitment to 'balance', the public service representation of such topics as domestic life, sexuality and political dissent is perceived by some audiences as too timid. It is routinely thought that certain things cannot be transmitted, or not in a particular way; or that when they are transmitted, their troublesome or outrageous implications are choked off. The sense that public service media are prone to 'bias' is further reinforced by the fact that public service media – here they are no different from their commercial competitors – unevenly distribute entitlements to speak and to be heard and seen. They too develop a cast of regulars – presenters, reporters, academic experts, professionals, politicians, businesspeople, showbiz figures – whose regular appearance on the media enables them to function as accredited representatives of public experience. The combined outcome of these corseting effects is to decrease the legitimacy of public service media. Audiences tend to become restless; as broadcasters know, they gradually lose their 'ontological' status by becoming less predictable in their tastes and more receptive of commercial forms of media.[8]

(3)   Technological change: A third difficulty faced by the public service model – the advent of cable, satellite television, community radio and computerized networks – is arguably the most serious, since it has destroyed the traditional belief that the scarcity of available spectrum blesses public service broadcasting with the status of a 'natural monopoly' within the boundaries of a given territorial nation-state. Contemporary technological change is not simply encircling public service broadcasting and forcing it to compete with privately owned firms within a multichannel environment. Less obviously, it is exposing the spatial metaphor deeply encoded within the public sector model, according to which citizens, acting within an integrated public sphere, properly belong to a carefully defined territory guarded by the sovereign nation-state, itself positioned within a wider, englobing system of territorially defined states.

The assumption that public service media properly function as servants and guarantors of territorially fixed nation-states preserved intact a similar geographic metaphor encoded within nationally demarcated systems of print journalism (as Benedict Anderson's study of print capitalism and nation-states has shown).[9] This metaphor nevertheless had to be fought for politically during the infant stage of broadcasting, as evidenced not only in the global struggle of European fascism and Soviet communism to tailor radio and film to their respective expansionist states, but also in the desperate efforts of early public service broadcasters to justify publicly why broadcasting media could be organized in a 'third way' – incorporating them into a parliamentary democratic state in which electronic media could serve to generate and sustain public life within a given territory. The famous document prepared for the Crawford Committee in 1925 by John Reith, the first

[8] See I. Ang, *Desperately Seeking the Audience* (London, 1991).
[9] Benedict Anderson, *Imagined Communities: Reflections on the Origin and Spread of Nationalism* (London, 1982).

director-general of the BBC, made the point explicitly. Public service broadcasting, Reith argued, should function as a national service. It should act as a powerful means of social unity, binding together the groups, regions and classes of civil society through the live relaying of national events, such as the first broadcast by King George V at the previous year's Empire Exhibition, which had the effect of 'making the nation as one man'.[10] A half-century later, Sir Michael Swann, chairman of the BBC's Board of Governors, argued before the Annan Committee that an 'enormous amount of the BBC's work was in fact social cement of one sort or another. Royal occasions, religious services, sports coverage and police series all reinforce the sense of belonging to our country, being involved in its celebrations and accepting what it stands for.'[11]

Still today this same assumption that the public service model is the principal forum which enables the whole nation to talk to itself is sometimes stated explicitly, as when French Presidents dub their television and radio services 'the voice of France' and BBC policy documents reiterate the principle that 'publicly funded broadcasters have a primary obligation to the public' and style the corporation as 'the national instrument of broadcasting'. The point is echoed in virtually every recent academic study of the public service/public sphere nexus.[12]

A revised theory of civil society must recognize that such talk – the talk of those who suppose an elective affinity between public service broadcasting and 'the public sphere' – is

---

[10] John Reith, 'Memorandum of Information on the Scope and Conduct of the Broadcasting Service', BBC Written Archives (Caversham, 1922, 1925), p. 4.

[11] Annan Committee, *Report of the Committee on the Future of Broadcasting* (London, 1977), p. 263.

[12] See Bernhard Peters, 'Der Sinn von Öffentlichkeit', *Kölner Zeitschrift für Soziologie und Sozialpsychologie*, vol. 34 (1994), pp. 42–76; James Curran, 'Rethinking the Media as a Public Sphere', in Peter Dahlgren and Colin Sparks (eds), *Communication and Citizenship: Journalism and the Public Sphere in the New Media Age* (London and New York, 1991), pp. 27–57; and Paddy Scannell, 'Public Service Broadcasting and Modern Public Life', *Media, Culture and Society*, vol. 11, no. 2 (1989), pp. 135–66.

hardening into dogma, precisely because the leading spatial metaphor upon which it rests is now out of touch with long-term media trends in the old parliamentary democracies. We are living in times in which spatial frameworks of communication are in a state of upheaval. The old dominance of state-structured and territorially bounded public life mediated by radio, television, newspapers and books is coming to an end. Its hegemony is rapidly being eroded by the development of a multiplicity of networked spaces of communication which are not tied immediately to territory, and which therefore irreversibly outflank and fragment anything formerly resembling a single, spatially integrated public sphere within a nation-state framework. The ideal of a unified public sphere and its corresponding vision of a territorially bounded republic of citizens striving to live up to their definition of the public good are obsolete. In their place, figuratively speaking, public life is today subject to 'refeudalization', not in the sense in which Habermas's *Strukturwandel der Öffentlichkeit* used the term, but in the different sense of modularization, of the development of a complex mosaic of differently sized, overlapping and interconnected public spheres that force us radically to revise our understanding of public life and its 'partner' terms, such as public opinion, the public good and the public/private distinction.

*   *   *

Although these public spheres emerge within differently-sized milieux within the nooks and crannies of civil societies and states, all of them are stages of power- and interest-bound action that display the essential characteristics of a public sphere. A public sphere is a particular type of spatial relationship between two or more people, usually connected by a certain means of communication (television, radio, satellite, fax, telephone, email, etc.), in which non-violent controversies erupt, for a brief or more extended period of time, concerning the power relations operating within their given milieu of interaction and/or within the wider milieux of social and political structures within which the disputants are situated. A public sphere has the effect of desacralizing power relationships. It is the vital medium of naming the unnameable, pointing at frauds, taking sides, starting arguments, inducing *diffidenza* (Eco), shaking the world, stopping it from falling asleep. Public spheres in this sense never appear in pure form – the following description is *idealtypisch* – and they rarely appear in isolation. Although they typically have a networked, interconnected character, contemporary public spheres have a fractured quality which is not being overcome by some broader trend towards an integrated public sphere. The examples selected below illustrate their heterogeneity and variable size, and that is why I choose, at the risk of being misunderstood, to distinguish among *micro-public spheres* in which there are dozens, hundreds or thousands of disputants interacting mainly at the sub-state level; *meso-public spheres* which normally comprise millions of people interacting at the level of the territorial nation-state framework; and *macro-public spheres* which normally encompass hundreds of millions and even billions of people enmeshed in disputes at the supranational and global levels of power. I should like to examine each in turn – and to explore their implications for a revised political theory of the role of public spheres within a civil society and democratic republic.

* * *

The coffeehouse, town-level meeting and literary circle, in which early modern public spheres developed, today find their counterparts in a wide variety of local spaces in which citizens enter into disputes about who does and who ought to get what, when and how. John Fiske's research has made a convincing case for the importance of bottom-up, small-scale locales in which citizens forge their identities, often in opposition to top-down 'imperializing' powers bent on regulating, redefining or extinguishing (or 'stationing') public life at the local level.[13] While Fiske (following Foucault) correctly emphasizes that these micro-public spheres take advantage of the fact that all large-scale institutions ultimately rest on the cooperation of their subordinates, and that challenges and

[13] John Fiske, *Power Plays, Power Works* (London, 1993).

changes at the micro level therefore necessarily have broader macro effects, he underestimates the broader political impor- tance of internal disputes within these locales. He instead pre- fers to emphasize the contestatory relationship between 'imperializing power' and locales, which has the unfortunate effect of ignoring the rich significance of these localized dis- putes for the conventional theory of the public sphere. Two examples will help to clarify these points – and to illustrate what is meant by a micro-public sphere.

Micro-public spheres are today a vital feature of all social movements. As Paul Mier, Alberto Mclucci and others have observed, contemporary social movements are less preoccu- pied with struggles over the production and distribution of material goods and resources, and more concerned with the ways in which post-industrial societies generate and withhold information and produce and sustain meanings among their members.[14] The organizations of the women's movement, for instance, not only raise important questions about the mater- ial inequalities suffered by women. They also, at the same time, challenge dominant masculinist codes by signalling to the rest of civil society the importance of symbolically recognizing differences. While the movements have millenarian tenden- cies, their concentration upon defining and redefining sym- bolic differences ensures that they are not driven by grand visions of a future utopian order. The supporters and sympa- thizers and actors within the movements are 'nomads of the present'. They focus upon the present, wherein they practise the future social changes they seek, and their organizational means are therefore valued as ends in themselves. Social move- ments normally comprise low-profile networks of small groups, organizations, initiatives, local contacts and friendships sub- merged in the everyday life patterns of civil society. These submerged networks, noted for their stress on solidarity, individual needs and part-time involvement, constitute the laboratories in which new experiences are invented and

[14] Alberto Melucci, *Nomads of the Present: Social Movements and Individual Needs in Contemporary Society*, ed. John Keane and Paul Mier (London and Philadelphia, 1989).

popularized. Within these local laboratories, movements utilize a variety of means of communication (telephones, faxes, photocopiers, camcorders, videos, personal computers) to question and transform the dominant codes of everyday life. These laboratories function as public spaces in which the elements of everyday life are mixed, remixed, developed and tested. Such public spheres as the discussion circle, the publishing house, the church, the clinic and a political chat over a drink with friends or acquaintances are the sites in which citizens question the pseudo-imperatives of reality and counter them with alternative experiences of time, space and interpersonal relations. On occasion, these public spheres coalesce into publicly visible media events, such as demonstrations in favour of gay male and lesbian rights or sit-ins against road-building or power plant projects. But, paradoxically, these micro-public spheres draw their strength from the fact that they are mostly latent. Although they appear to be 'private', acting at a distance from official public life, party politics and the glare of media publicity, they in fact display all the characteristics of small group public efforts, whose challenging of the existing distribution of power can be effective exactly because they operate unhindered in the unnewsworthy nooks and crannies of civil society.

Micro-public spheres may also be developing among children within households, as the contentious growth during the 1980s of a video games culture illustrates. For many adults, particularly those without children, the widespread appeal of video games during that period remains incomprehensible; contemplating a four-button keypad leaves them with a powerful sense of wasted time, ignorance based upon innocence, even disgust at the thought that the current generation of children will grow up as the first ever in modern times to learn to compute before they learn to read and write. But for most children, at least most boys between eight and eighteen, the past decade's experience of playing video games and creating an everyday culture of classroom stories, swapping and sharing videos, and a new critical lexicon (filled with codewords like 'cool', 'crap', 'smelly' and 'cacky') that generates tensions with adults became a routine part of childhood – as routine as old-fashioned ways of hating parents or squashing a worm or overfeeding a goldfish to death. The last decade's growth within households of micro-public spheres of this kind proved to be dramatic. During the highpoint of growth in the United Kingdom in the early 1990s, for example, the video games market, dominated by the Japanese companies Sega and Nintendo, grew from virtually nothing to a turnover of around £800 million per annum. Eight out of ten children between eleven and fourteen came to play video games; six out of ten had their own game consoles (the hardware needed to play games on television monitors); while in 1992 alone, around two million new consoles were sold.

Industry figures and their critics like to cite the power of the advertising 'hook' to explain their marketing success, but this underestimates the way in which during the past decade the popularity of video games among children is chosen by subjects striving, if only intuitively, for the power to co-determine the outcomes of their electronically mediated play. It is true that the marketed form of video games normally thwarted children's choices. The sex-typing of women as figures who are acted upon, and often victimized as kidnap victims in need of rescue, was a typical case in point.[15] Video games nevertheless challenged children to come to terms with the new media of digital communication – preparing the way for the current vigorous expansion of what might be called the CD-ROM culture. The appeal of these new media stems not only from the fact that for brief moments children can escape the demands of household and school by becoming part of an alternative world of bionic men, damsels in distress, lion kings, world explorers, galactic invasions and teenage mutant turtles. Video games and CD-ROMs also promise interactivity and actually encourage users to improve their hand–eye coordination and interpretative skills by browsing through texts in an orderly but non-sequential manner. Unlike the process of learning to read books, which reduces children initially to mere readers with little freedom but that of accepting or rejecting the rules

[15] E.F. Provenzo, *Video Kids: Making Sense of Nintendo* (Cambridge, Mass. and London, 1991).

of a text, the playing of digital games confronts children with a form of hypertext.[16] Players are required to choose their own pathways through texts composed of blocks of words, images and sounds that are linked electronically by multiple paths, chains or trails that are unfinished and open-ended. Digital games blur the boundaries between readers and writers by encouraging their users to determine how they move through a forest of possibilities to do with rescue and revenge, and good versus evil, constrained only by the permitted household rules governing playtime, the manufacturers' *mise en scène*, and the child's capacity for inventiveness in the face of persistent adult suspicion or outright opposition to the phenomenon.

*   *   *

The treatment of *meso-public spheres* can be comparatively brief, since they are the most familiar of the three types of public sphere examined here. Meso-public spheres are those spaces of controversy about power that encompass millions of people watching, listening or reading across vast distances. They are mainly coextensive with the territorial state, but they may also extend beyond its boundaries to encompass neighbouring audiences (as in the case of German-language programming and publishing in Austria); their reach may also be limited to regions within states, as in the case of the non-Castilian-speaking regions of Spain like Catalonia and the Basque country. Meso-public spheres are mediated by large-circulation newspapers such as the *New York Times, Le Monde, die Zeit*, the *Globe and Mail*, and the Catalan daily, *Avui*. They are also mediated by electronic media such as BBC radio and television, Swedish Radio, RAI and (in the United States) National Public Radio and the four national networks (CBS, NBC, ABC and Fox).

Although constantly pressured 'from below' by micro-public spheres, meso-public spheres display considerable tenacity. There is no necessary zero-sum relationship between these differently sized public domains, in part because each feeds

---

[16] T.H. Nelson, *Computer Lib: Dream Machines* (Redmond, 1987).

upon tensions with the other (readers of national newspapers, for instance, may and do consult locally produced magazines or bulletins, precisely because of their different themes and emphases); and in part because meso-public spheres thrive upon media which appeal to particular national or regional language groupings, and which have well-established and powerful production and distribution structures that sustain their proven ability to circulate to millions of people certain types of news, current affairs, films and entertainment that daily reinforce certain styles and habits of communication about matters of public concern. The strength of reputation, funding and distribution is certainly an important reason why public service media, notwithstanding their self-commercialization, are unlikely to disappear as props of public life. There is another, more surprising reason why public life at the meso-level is unlikely to disappear. The above-mentioned examples of the media sustaining meso-public spheres highlight the point – foreign to recent attempts to tie the theory of the public sphere to the fate of public service media – that public controversies about power are also regularly facilitated by privately controlled media of civil society. There is plenty of evidence that, just as public service media are ever more subject to market forces, market-led media are subject to a long-term process of self-politicization, in the sense that they are forced to address matters of concern to citizens capable of distinguishing between market 'hype' and public controversies. The entry into official politics of commercial media figures such as Ronald Reagan and Silvio Berlusconi are extreme instances of this trend. The British tabloids' ruthless probing of the private lives of monarchs and politicians during the past decade is symptomatic of the same trend. So also are popular current affairs programmes such as CNN's *Larry King Live* and the remarkable proliferation of fast-cut television talk shows like *Ricki Lake*, which, amid advertisements for commodities such as mouthwash, chocolates, inner-spring mattresses and pizza, simulate raucous domestic quarrels about such matters as teenage sex, pregnancy and child abuse, in front of selected audiences who argue bitterly among themselves and, amid uproar, talk back to the presenter, experts

and interviewees, contradicting their views, calling them 'real
asses', urging them to 'get real' and insisting that something
or other 'sucks with a capital S'.

* * *

The recent growth of *macro-public spheres* at the global or regional (e.g., European Union) level is among the most striking, least researched developments running contrary to the
orthodox theory of the public sphere. Macro-publics of hundreds of millions of citizens are the (unintended) consequence
of the international concentration of mass media firms previously owned and operated at the territorial nation-state level.
A prior form of concentration of media capital has, of course,
been under way for a century, especially in the magazine and
newspaper industries and in the core group of news agencies,
dominated by American, British, German and French firms
that carved up the world within the spheres of influence of
their respective governments. The current globalization of
media firms represents a projection of this process of concentration on to the international plane. It involves the chain
ownership and cross-ownership of newspapers, the acquisi-
tion of media by ordinary industrial concerns and, significantly,
the regional and global development of satellite-linked communications systems.

The development of globe-girdling communications firms
such as News Corporation International, Reuters, Time-Warner
and Bertelsmann was not driven by the motive of funding the
development of international publics. Although research on
the perceived motives and benefits of globalization remains
limited, it is clear that the process, which is virtually without
historical precedents, is driven by reasons of political economy.
Media firms operating at the global level have certain advantages over their nationally based counterparts. Headed by a
tiny group of people who have become adept at 'turning
around' ailing media firms and fully utilizing their assets,
transnational firms take advantage of economies of scale. They
are able to shift resources of expertise, marketing skills and
journalistic talent, for instance, from one part of the media
field to another; they can also reduce costs and innovate by

tapping the specialist workforces of various societies. These firms can also effect synergies of various kinds, such as trying out a novel in one country and producing a movie based upon it in another, or releasing a work successively through such media as cable, video, television, magazines and paperback books, without the difficult rights-negotiation and scheduling problems that inevitably arise when a diversity of competing national companies is involved. Highly important as well is the advantageous fact that transnational media firms are often able to evade nation-state regulations and shift the core energies of the whole operation from one market to another as political and legal and cultural climates change.

Among the central ironies of this risk-driven, profit-calculating process is its nurturing of the growth of publics stretching beyond the boundaries of the territorial nation-state. Most of these public spheres are so far fledglings. They operate briefly and informally – they have few guaranteed sources of funding and legal protection, and are therefore highly fragile, often fleeting phenomena. International media events, which are now staged virtually several times every week, are cases in point. As Daniel Dayan and Elihu Katz, Daniel Hallin and others have shown, global media events like summits are highly charged symbolic processes covered by the entire media of the world and addressed primarily to a fictive 'world audience'.[17] In the three major summits hosted by Reagan and Gorbachev – at Geneva in 1985, Washington in 1987 and Moscow in 1988 – audiences straddling the globe watched as media channels such as CNN, ABC's *Nightline* and the Soviet morning programme *90 Minutes* relayed versions of a summit that signalled the end of the Cold War. It is commonly objected that such coverage spreads rituals of pacification, rendering global audiences mute in their fascination with the spectacle of the event. That could indeed be legitimately said of the heavily censored Malvinas War and Gulf War coverage,

---

[17] Daniel Dayan and Elihu Katz, *Media Events: The Live Broadcasting of History* (Cambridge, Mass., 1992); and Daniel C. Hallin, *We Keep America On Top of the World: Television Journalism and the Public Sphere* (London and New York, 1994).

but still there are signs that the globalcasting of summits and other events tends to be conducted in the subjunctive tense, in that they heighten audiences' sense that the existing 'laws' of power politics are far from 'natural' and that the shape of the world is therefore dependent in part on current efforts to refashion it according to certain criteria.

The dramatic emphasis upon the subjunctive, combined with the prospect of reaching a worldwide audience, can incite new public controversies about power stretching beyond the limited boundaries of meso-public spheres. During the Reagan–Gorbachev summits, for example, political arguments about the dangerous proliferation of nuclear and conventional weaponry were commonplace among the citizens and governments of various countries at the same time; and in the Soviet Union, where autonomous public life had long been considered a counter-revolutionary crime, the supporters of Boris Yeltsin were heartened by the way in which the demoted party leader's interviews with CBS and the BBC during the Moscow summit forced Mikhail Gorbachev to respond with a televised press conference; meanwhile, Soviet religious dissidents successfully lobbied President Reagan to grant them a public meeting, at which there was a frank airing of conflicting views about elections, the future of religion and the comparative 'standards of living' of America and the Soviet Union.

*   *   *

Probably the most dramatic example so far of the way in which global media events can and do incite public controversies about power before audiences of hundreds of millions of people is the crisis in Tiananmen Square in China during the late spring of 1989. Broadcast live by CNN, twenty-four hours a day, the Tiananmen episode was a turning point in the development of global news. It was not only perceived as the most important news story yet to be covered by international satellite television. It was also (according to Lewis Friedland and others[18]) the first occasion ever when satellite television

[18] Lewis A. Friedland, *Covering the World: International Television News Services* (New York, 1992).

directly shaped the events themselves, which unfolded rapidly on three planes: within national boundaries, throughout global diplomatic circles, and on the stage of international public arguments about how to resolve the crisis. CNN's wire-service-like commitment to bring its viewers all significant stories from all sides of the political spectrum helped to publicize the demands of the students, many of whom had travelled abroad and understood well the political potential of the television medium in establishing public spheres in opposition to the totalitarian Chinese state. Not coincidentally, they chose 'The Goddess of Democracy' as their central symbol, while their placards carried quotations from Abraham Lincoln and others, all in English for the benefit of western audiences. The students reckoned, accurately, that by keeping the cameras and cellular telephones (and, later, 8 mm 'handicams' carried around on bicycles) trained on themselves they would maximize the chances of their survival and international recognition. Their cause certainly won international recognition from other states and citizens. By damaging the international reputation of the Party, the global coverage of the Tiananmen events may also have boosted the long-term chances of a non-violent self-dismantling of the communist regime (along the lines of Kádar's Hungary). In the short run, the coverage almost certainly prolonged the life of the protest, which ended in the massacre of between 400 and 800 students. According to CNN's Alec Miran, who was executive producer in China during the crisis, 'People were coming up to us in the street, telling us to "Keep going, keep broadcasting, that they won't come in while you're on the air." That turned out to be true. The troops went in after our cameras were shut down.'[19]

* * *

The pathbreaking development during the past two decades of an international system of computerized communications networks provides a final illustration of macro-public spheres. Based upon such techniques as packet switching developed during the 1960s by the Advanced Research Projects Agency

[19] Cited in ibid., p. 5.

(ARPA) for the United States Department of Defense, a world-wide network of computers funded by governments, businesses, universities and citizens is beginning to draw together users from all continents and walks of life. The Internet, the most talked about and talked through network, comprises an estimated 5 million computers serving as hosts that are in turn directly connected to millions of other computers used by up to 50 million people. The number of Internet 'citizens' is growing rapidly (by an estimated 1–2 million users a month), partly because of heavy subsidies that keep access costs to a minimum, partly because of peer pressure to get an e-mail address and partly because of the lack of constraints, globality and informality currently enjoyed by users communicating for a variety of self-chosen ends. Some 'surf' the Internet, logging on to servers throughout the world just for the hell of it. Companies and other organizations conduct banking transactions and transmit financial and administrative data by means of it. Live telecasts of speeches and transmissions of scanned images of weather maps, paintings and nude photographs are commonplace. Still others use the 'Net' to obtain detailed print-outs of data downloaded from libraries or to 'chat' with a friend on another continent.

The manifold purposes for which the Internet can be used at reasonable cost or free of charge has led some observers to liken its users, in neo-Romantic terms, to eighteenth-century travellers seeking food and shelter in houses they reach at night-fall.[20] While correctly drawing attention to the contractual or voluntary character of electronic interactions, the simile is arguably misplaced. It not merely understates the way in which the often clumsy organization of information sources generates confusion among users who are posting items – with the consequence that travellers on the information highway find themselves hazy about their routes, their means of travel, their hosts' house rules and (insofar as messages are frequently forwarded several times, often by unknown receiver/senders) their ultimate destinations. More pertinent is the fact that the simile

---

[20] Ed Krol, *The Whole Internet: Users' Guide and Catalogue* (Sebastopol, Calif., 1991).

fails because the Internet stimulates the growth of macro-public spheres. There is a category of users with a 'net presence' who utilize the medium not as travellers but as citizens, who generate controversies with other members of a far-flung 'imagined community' about matters of power and principle. The Association for Progressive Communications (APC), for example, functions as a worldwide partnership of member networks dedicated to providing low-cost and advanced computer communications services for the purpose of network strengthening and information sharing among organizations and individuals working for environmental sustainability, economic and social justice, and human rights. Within the APC framework, spheres of public controversy ('public discussion forums') stretching to all four corners of the earth have a permanent presence. So too do reflections upon the power relations operating within the global networks themselves. 'Netizens', whose approach to the public forums of the Internet exudes selfishness – taking rather than giving – can generally expect to be abused ('flamed'), as unsolicited advertisers find to their embarrassment. Controversies are erupting about the merits of state-subsidized, cost-free access of citizens to the Internet; proposals are surfacing (in the United States) for the formation of a Corporation for Public Cybercasting that would serve as a clearing house for federal funds, help to increase the density and tensility of the network, and lobby for citizens' access; and fears are expressed that the telecommunications and entertainment industries are building advanced communications systems that would enable them to control parts of the Internet and thereby levy considerably higher access charges.

*   *   *

The above attempt radically to rethink the theory of the public sphere, like all lines of enquiry that transgress the limits of conventional wisdom, opens up new bundles of complex questions with important implications for both the interpretation of civil society and future research in the fields of politics and communications. The most obvious implication is that the neo-republican attempt to tie the theory of the public sphere to the institution of public service broadcasting has failed on empirical and normative grounds, and that, more positively, there are empirical reasons alone why the concept of 'public spheres' should be brought to bear on phenomena as disparate as computer networking, citizens' initiatives, newspaper circulation, satellite broadcasting and children playing digital games. Public spheres are not exclusively 'housed' within state-protected public service media; nor (contrary to Habermas and others) are they somehow tied by definition to what has been called *political society*: that is, to the zone of social life narrowly wedged between the world of power and money (state/economy) and the prepolitical group associations of civil society.[21] The concept of 'political society' is an outdated eighteenth- and nineteenth-century fiction. And the political geography supposed by both the Habermasian and public service model theories of 'the public sphere' is inadequate. Public spheres can and do develop within various realms of civil society and state institutions, including within the supposed enemy territory of consumer markets and within the world of power that lies beyond the reach of territorial nation-states, the Hobbesian world conventionally dominated by shadowy agreements, suited diplomacy, business transactions, and war and rumours of war.

* * *

Whether or not there is a long-term modern tendency for public spheres to spread into areas of life previously immune from controversies about power is necessarily a subject for a larger enquiry. Yet among the implications of this reflection upon the theme of public life in the old democracies is the fact that there are no remaining areas of social or political life automatically protected against public controversies about the distribution of power. The early modern attempt to represent patterns of property ownership, market conditions, household life and events like birth and death as 'natural' is gradually

---

[21] The concept of political society, contrasted with civil society and drawn from Alexis de Tocqueville and others, is defended in Jean L. Cohen and Andrew Arato, *Civil Society and Political Theory* (Cambridge, Mass. and London, 1994), pp. 78–81.

withering away. So too is the older, originally Greek assumption that the public sphere of citizenship necessarily rests on the tight-lipped privacy (literally, the idiocy) of the *oikos*. As the process of mediated publicity spreads – television talk shows like *Ricki Lake* and children playing digital games suggest – supposedly private phenomena are being drawn into the vortices of negotiated controversy that are the hallmark of public spaces. The realm of privacy – supposed by Hegel and others to be the hidden foundation of modern civil societies – is disappearing. The process of politicization undermines the conventionally accepted division between 'the public' (where power controversies are reckoned to be the legitimate business of others) and 'the private' (where such controversy is said to have no legitimate role before the thrones of 'intimacy' or individual choice or God-given or biological 'naturalness'). Politicization exposes the arbitrariness or conventionalism of traditional definitions of 'the private', making it harder (as various figures of power are today painfully learning) to justify any action as a private matter. Paradoxically, the same process of politicization also triggers a new category of public disputes about the merits of defining or redefining certain zones of social and political life as 'private' – and therefore as nobody else's business. Legal authorities publicize the problem of rape while insisting upon the need to keep private the identities of those who have suffered the crime; gay males and lesbians campaign publicly for their right to live without intrusions by bigots and gawking journalists; advocates of the right to privacy press publicly for data protection legislation; meanwhile, embattled politicians and scandalized monarchs insist publicly that the media have no place in their bedrooms.

* * *

Such developments cannot adequately be understood from within the orthodox perspective on the public sphere, wedded as it is to a version of the early modern division between 'the public' and 'the private'. Its defenders might reply that at least some of the public spheres mentioned above are bogus public spheres, in that they are neither permanent nor structured by rational argumentation, or what Garnham calls 'a rational and universalistic politics'. Certainly – as the *impermanent* public controversy generated by social movements shows – not all the examples of public life cited above display longevity, but that arguably signals the need to question the conventional assumption that a public sphere is only a public sphere insofar as it persists through time. Within actually existing civil societies, public spheres tend increasingly to be evanescent. The point about rational argumentation is more difficult to answer, although it is again clear that there is no reason in principle why the concept of the public sphere must necessarily be wedded to the ideal of communication orientated towards reaching consensus based upon the force of the best argument (or what Habermas calls *verständigungsorientierten Handelns*).[22] In their study of television talk shows, Sonia Livingstone and Peter Lunt usefully highlight the several ways in which audience discussion programmes defy the dominant philosophical notion of rationality, derived from deductive logic, according to which there exists a set of formal reasoning procedures that express tacit inference rules concerning the truth or falsity of assertions independently of the content or context of utterances.[23] Following Wittgenstein's *Philosophische Untersuchungen*, Livingstone and Hunt defend the legitimacy of lay or 'ordinary reasoning', such as quarrels (characterized by emotional intensity and a commitment to assert one's point of view at all costs) and preaching, political oratory and story-telling, in which points are built up in a haphazard manner by layering, recursion, and repetition. Their move is convincing, but their conclusions remain a trifle too rationalist. Early modern public spheres – as I proposed from a post-Weberian perspective in *Public Life and Late Capitalism*, and

---

[22] Jürgen Habermas, 'Was heisst Universalpragmatik?', in Karl-Otto Apel (ed.), *Sprachpragmatik und Philosophie* (Frankfurt am Main, 1976). Compare Craig Calhoun, 'Civil Society and the Public Sphere', op. cit., p. 279, where a public sphere is said to 'represent the potential for the people organized in civil society to alter their own conditions of existence by means of rational-critical discourse'.

[23] Sonia Livingstone and Peter Lunt, *Talk on Television: Audience Participation and Public Debate* (London, 1991); see also Joshua Gamson, *Freaks Talk Back* (Chicago, 1998).

Oskar Negt and Alexander Kluge insisted from a neo-Marxian standpoint[24] – did not conform to the Habermasian *idealtyp* of rational discussion. Music, opera, sport, painting and dancing were among the forms of communication propelling the growth of civil society and public life, and there is therefore no principled reason, aside from philosophical prejudice, why their late-twentieth-century popular counterparts – the rambunctiousness of MTV's annual video-awards, the simulated uproar of *Ricki Lake* shows or the hypertext of digital games – should not be understood as legitimate potential media of power conflicts.

*   *   *

To suppose that public controversies about power can and should unfold by means of a variety of modes of communication is not to fall into the relativist trap of concluding that any and every power struggle counts as a legitimate public sphere. Violent confrontation among subjects does not do so, since, as the originally Greek understanding of war as external to the *polis* maintained, it seeks physically to silence or destroy outright its antagonists. The essential point is this: the plea for a pluralistic understanding of the variable forms of communication that currently constitute public life shares an elective affinity with a non-foundationalist understanding of democracy as a type of regime which enables a genuine plurality of individuals and groups within civil society openly to express their solidarity with, or opposition to, others' ideals and forms of life. By abandoning the futile and often dangerous high roads of supposed transhistorical Ideals and definite Truths, the plea for a pluralistic account of public life implies that there is no ultimate criterion for determining which particular type of public controversy is universally preferable. The most that can be said, normatively speaking, is that a healthy democratic regime is one in which various types of public sphere are thriving, with no single one of them actually enjoying a monopoly

---

[24] Oskar Negt and Alexander Kluge, *Öffentlichkeit und Erfahrung: Zur Organisationsanalyse von bürgerlicher und proletarischer Öffentlichkeit* (Frankfurt am Main, 1972).

in public disputes about the distribution of power. In contrast, a regime dominated by television talk shows or by spectacular media events would compromise its citizens' integrity. It might prove to be as stifling as a regime in which seminar-style 'rational discussion' or demagogic political preaching served as the sole 'civilized' standard of disputation about who gets what, when and how.

*   *   *

The emphasis here upon pluralism brings us back to the subject of space, which was the point of departure of this broad reconsideration of the structural transformations of the public sphere in the old democracies. Within the republican tradition of political thinking that extends through to the recent attempt to tie public life to the public service model, it is normally assumed that power is best monitored and its abuse most effectively checked by means of ongoing argumentation within the territorial framework of the nation-state. Republicanism supposes that public-spirited citizens can best act together within an integrated, politically constructed space that is ultimately rooted in the physical place occupied by state power. This supposition needs to be rejected, since a growing number of public spheres – the Internet and global media events, for instance – are politically constructed spaces that have no immediate connection with physical territory. Public life, one could say, is presently subject to a process of deterritorialization which ensures that citizens' shared sense of proximity to one another in various milieux bears ever less relationship to the places where they were actually born, where they grew up, fell in love, worked and lived, and where they will eventually die.

*   *   *

It might be objected that the attempt to categorize contemporary public life into spaces of varying scope or 'reach' is mistaken on both empirical and normative grounds. Empirically speaking, it could be said that the public spheres discussed above are not discrete spaces, as the categories micro-, meso- and macro-public sphere imply; that they rather resemble a modular system of overlapping networks defined by the lack of differentiation among spheres. Certainly, the concept of modularization serves as a useful reminder of the dangers of reifying the distinction among micro-, meso- and macro-public spheres. It is also helpful in understanding the growing complexity of contemporary public life. But this does not mean that the boundaries among variously sized public spheres are obliterated completely. To the contrary, modular systems thrive on internal differentiation, whose workings can thus be understood only by means of *idealtypisch* categories that highlight those systems' inner boundaries. The comparatively recent development of computerized communications is illustrative of this point. Computer networks originally linked terminals to mainframes for time sharing, but during the past two decades a pattern of distributed structures at the micro, meso and macro levels has come to predominate. During the 1980s, local area networks (LANs) providing high-speed data communication within an organization spread rapidly; they have subsequently been linked into metropolitan area networks (MANs) that are often associated with a 'teleport' of satellite dishes, and into wide area networks (WANs) that may cover several continents – and yet still the differentiation among micro/meso/macro domains remains a vital feature of the overall system.

* * *

The triadic distinction among differently sized public spheres can also be contested on normative grounds. During the early years of the twentieth century, at the beginning of the era of broadcasting, John Dewey's *The Public and Its Problems* (1927) famously expressed the outlines of the complaint that modern societies are marked by the fragmentation of public life. 'There are too many publics and too much of public concern for our existing resources to cope with', wrote Dewey. 'The essential need', he added, 'is the improvement of a unified system of methods and conditions of debate, discussion, and persuasion, *that* is the problem of the public.'[25] This kind of appeal (repeated more recently by Robert Bellah, Michael Sandel and others) to revive republicanism is questionable. It

[25] John Dewey, *The Public and Its Problems* (New York, 1927), p. 142.

fails to see that the structural differentiation of public spaces is unlikely to be undone in the coming decades, and that therefore the continued use of 'the' public sphere ideal is bound to empty it of empirical content and to turn the ideal into a nostalgic, unrealizable utopia. We are moving, as Henri Lefebvre predicted, from a society in which space is seen as an 'absolute' towards one in which there are ongoing 'trials of space'.[26] Orthodox republicanism also ignores the undemocratic implications of its own hankering after a unified public sphere. The supposition that all power disputes can ultimately be sited at the level of the territorially bounded nation-state is a remnant from the era of state building and the corresponding struggles of its inhabitants to widen the franchise – and, hence, to direct public controversies primarily at the operations of the sovereign state. In the present era of the universal franchise, by contrast, it is not so much who votes but *where* people vote that is becoming a central issue for democratic politics. From this perspective, the proliferation of mosaics of differently sized public spheres ought to be welcomed and practically reinforced by means of political struggle, law, money and improved modes of communication. Exactly because of their capacity to monitor the exercise of power from a variety of sites within state and civil society institutions, public spheres ensure that nobody 'owns' power and increase the likelihood that its exercise everywhere is rendered more accountable to those whom it directly or indirectly affects.

The trends described here are admittedly only trends. Within the old democracies, there are plenty of anti-democratic countertrends, and it should therefore not be supposed that we are at the beginning of the end of the era of unaccountable power. All political classes, Harold Innis once remarked, have sought to enhance their power by utilizing certain media of communication to define and to control the spaces in which their subjects live.[27] Statues of military and political heroes sited in public squares are only the most obvious example of a much older and highly complex history of rulers' attempts to

---

[26] Henri Lefebvre, *La Production de l'espace* (Paris, 1974), p. 116.
[27] Harold Innis, *The Bias of Communication* (Toronto, 1991).

define space in their honour, and thereby to inspire devotion among their subjects by making the exercise of power seem unblemished – and unchallengeable.

When reflecting upon the twentieth century, Innis doubted whether this struggle by dominant power groups to regulate their subjects' living space could be resisted. He supposed that space-biased media such as newspapers and radio broadcasting, despite their promise to democratize information, in fact entrench new modes of domination. Was Innis right in this global conviction? Is modernity, just like previous epochs, distinguished by dominant forms of media that absorb, record and transform information into systems of knowledge consonant with the dominant institutional power structures? Is the era that lies beyond public service broadcasting likely to prove unfriendly towards public life? Is the vision of a democratic plurality of public spheres nothing more than a bad utopia? Or is the future likely to see a variety of contradictory trends, including not only new modes of domination but also unprecedented public battles to define and to control the spaces in which citizens appear?

In present-day theorizations of civil society, such questions are at present poorly formulated, while the tentative answers they elicit are by definition either not yet available or highly speculative. Perhaps the most that can be said at present is that a theory of civil society and public life that clings dogmatically to the vision of a unified public sphere in which 'public opinion' and 'the public interest' are defined is a chimera – and that for the sake of democracy it ought now to be jettisoned.

Endings

It is only a decade ago that the eighteenth-century distinction between civil society and the state seemed anomalous, foreign, an object of cynicism, even of outright hostility. These reflections on civil society have shown how, in a wholly unexpected reversal of fortunes, this antiquated distinction has since become voguish among politicians, academics, journalists, business leaders, relief agencies and citizens' organizations. The various sources and phases of the dramatic worldwide popularization of the term have been examined. Its appearance in an extraordinary variety of different contexts – from China to Tunisia, from South Africa to the emerging European Union – has been mapped, and throughout attempts have been made to clarify as carefully as possible the different and conflicting grammars and vocabularies of the language of civil society. Considerable care has been taken to highlight the different possible meanings of the distinction between civil society and the state. The theoretical confusions, paradoxes, ironies and dangers presently lurking within this perspective have been of special interest. The advantages and disadvantages of life in a civil society have been charted. Efforts have been made as well to take the reader into previously unexplored intellectual territory by demonstrating that the civil society perspective contains unharnessed potentials – that it is possible to develop bold new images of civil society that alter the ways in which we think about such matters as power, property, nationalism, publicity and violence. And this study of civil

society has set out to do all these things in an unusual style –
by means of deliberately broken narratives and 'cubist' perspectives that have considerable resonance with the fractured,
dynamic quality of actually existing civil societies.

For those within the human sciences who remain fundamentally hostile towards the civil society perspective, or perhaps
just unconvinced or unmoved by its premises and promises, a
stroll through the bulldozed heart of a city like Beirut is strongly
recommended. The recommended journey is bound to batter
the visitor's senses with the nasty facts of a city badly scarred
by prolonged incivility. The visitor will learn at first hand what
happens when states collapse and (nascent) civil societies im-
plode. The visitor will naturally hear stories from those who
survived of the ways in which the conflict that racked Beirut
for nearly two decades had all the structural characteristics of
an *uncivil war*.[1] Experts will tell the visitor of the immense tasks
of social healing and postwar political reconstruction facing the
city, of how basic public services have been wrecked, and why
most of the population of Beirut today suffers in one way or
another from various forms of long-term physical, psychological, economic and ecological damage. But the visitor will learn
much more than such generalities. Bathed in brilliant Mediterranean sunshine, he or she will stroll to see and hear and smell
and taste and touch the dirty details of what happens when a
vibrant civil society is destroyed.

In this uncivil city the contradictoriness of daily life is as-
tonishing. The proud bells of the Catholic Church of St Francis
ring out in streets choked with rubbish. Boys in ragged trou-
sers, some limbless and disabled, kick footballs on makeshift
red earth pitches shaded by clumps of white-barked eucalyp-
tus unscarred by war. The visitor will see satellite dishes. Hill-
top mosques. Tooting taxis and jackhammers. Men gambling
at backgammon, sipping dark coffee in the shade. And, of
course, Syrian soldiers, dressed in red berets and AK47s, bayo-
nets fixed, watching and waiting, getting on with the job of
policing the new order, if order it can be called.

---

[1] See my *Reflections on Violence*, op. cit., pp. 131–3, 139–41; and the discussion of 'violence without victory' in Theodore Hanf, *Coexistence in Wartime
Lebanon* (london, 1993), chapter 5.

Over there is a sparkling new Pizza Hut. Smells of raw sewage come from another direction. At right angles are rusted-out Datsuns doubling as roadside stalls, stuffed with used blankets, brassware, buckets, brushes, bags, books. Here come youths on roller skates, zipping past pedestrians on crutches, missing limbs and limping. The visitor will be impressed by the local art of converting ripped-out car seats into street chairs. And by the fancy hotels guarded by men in white gloves and smart grey suits. There are wall poster pictures of unknown martyrs and well-known teachings of sheikhs preaching militancy. And the ubiquitous Coca-Cola billboards, rusted and shot-up, splattered with wartime graffiti: MR GO TO HELL GH+ST NASTY NIKE BOYS HAKIM BOOMBASTIC FUCK YOU BEVERLY HILLS DISIRE LAW=LIES.

This is a city in which giant rumbling Caterpillars and six-wheeled trucks belching black smoke overpower the laughter of children. They cough on choking dust, and are revived by whiffs of salty air from the putrid Mediterranean. Old men, young men push handcarts piled high with cardboard. Tangled nests of electrical and telephone wires clutter every street corner. Air France is overhead. So too are Israeli fighter jets. The empty banks meanwhile bulge with money. And there are high-rise condos with wishful names like Florida Tower and Mirage Plaza.

Dear traveller, do not forget to see the wrecked squalor of Sabra and Chatil. Listen there to the stories of cold-blooded murder of defenceless exiles. Then move on in shock and shame to other parts of the city. Sample the lemon juice stands. Look at the battered tyres piled high on oil-soaked pavements. Witness the army of second-hand demolition cranes skilled at pounding twisted and broken buildings day and night, finishing off the job begun by the masked men with bazookas. Climb the skylines of rubble. Here and there spot a fig or almond sapling fighting for its right to survive. Admire the workmen perched on scaffolding, chiselling, sweating, trying to rescue walls not earmarked for levelling. Observe the half-camouflaged green tanks. Mobile phones. Tar-splattered alleycats. Veils. Moustaches. Parisian fashion. And the rubbish sorters who search for matching shoes buried in offal and rotting vegetables.

The bourgeois shops selling the spoils of war are not to be missed: the visitor can buy brass beds, silver platters, gold rings, chandeliers, nineteenth-century English paintings. Around the corner, up on a grassless knoll, are fused metal minarets gutted by gunfire. Explore the heaps of white concrete pipes. Talk to the archaeologists who are digging deep to bury the recent past. Then it will be time for a stroll on the kitsch esplanade: traffic jams, ferris wheels, families slurping ice cream, young boys holding hands, Mortal Kombat arcades, cafés where young women relax, veiled and unveiled together, all smoking Marlboro. And lucky visitor, please don't miss the blue-fronted Holiday Inn, the uncivil city's tallest building: moon-cratered and shell-blackened walls, see-through floors, a 25-storey corpse flanked by twisted metal, heaped debris and hunchbacked men rummaging for a future, with shrieking swallows circling overhead.

Index

I am most grateful to Patrick Burke for compiling this index and for assisting my research when writing other sections of the book.   J. K.